Child Labour in India

Challenges for Theological Thinking and
Christian Ministry in India

Holistic Child Development Series

Child Labour in India

Challenges for Theological Thinking and Christian Ministry in India

Rohan P. Gideon

ISPCK / NCCI
2011

Child Labour in India : *Challenges for Theological Thinking and Christian Ministry in India -* Jointly published by Rev. Dr. Ashish Amos of Indian Society for Promoting Christian Knowledge (ISPCK), Post Box 1585, 1654, Madarsa Road, Kashmere Gate, Delhi-110006, for National Council Churches of India (NCCI) Nagpur - 440 001 under the Holistic Child Development Series (HCDS).

The views expressed in the book are those of the author and the publisher takes no responsibility for any of the statements.

This book in its original form is the thesis submitted to the Senate of Serampore College towards the degree of M. Th. and is published with written permission.

The author is responsible for the title, contents and opinions expressed in it.

ISBN: 978-81-8465-139-3

Laser typeset by

ISPCK, Post Box 1585, 1654, Madarsa Road, Kashmere Gate, Delhi-110006 • *Tel:* 23866323

e-mail: ashish@ispck.org.in • ella@ispck.org.in
website: www.ispck.org.in

Contents

Acknowledgements

I am extremely grateful to God for being the source of wisdom, knowledge and good health all through, especially during the time spent on doing this project. Also, it is with great joy that I acknowledge the kindness and goodwill of many people in bringing out this book.

The publication of this work was possible when Mr. Christopher Rajkumar, Executive Secretary, Commission for Justice, Peace and Creation of National Council of Churches in India, identified my work under the Commission's auspices for Campaign on Child Rights and its objective to develop awareness and corresponding theological resources. This assistance corresponds with the NCCI's centenary celebrations' publications and the Commission's solidarity with the wronged-against. Dr. Mar Atsongchanger, Secretary-Communications & Relations, NCCI, graciously consented that NCCI be a joint publisher with ISPCK for this book.

I am especially grateful to Rev. Dr. Roger Gaikwad, General Secretary, NCCI, and Child-rights Theologian-Activist, for writing the foreword for this book.

Also, my wife, Chitra, and son, Pranay, gave me the much-needed co-operation, refreshing distraction and intellectual environment. I am also grateful to my parents, my sister's family, my in-laws and many other members of my family for being a big source of encouragement.

This work in its original form was my M. Th. thesis submitted to the Federated Faculty for Research in Religion and Culture, Kottayam, Kerala, in 2008. I am grateful to my supervisor, Fr. Dr. K. M. George, Professor of Theology and Principal of the Orthodox Theological Seminary, Kottayam, for his incisive observations and comments on my thesis. Prof. A. K. Ramakrishnan, Professor of International Relations and Politics, M. G. University, Kottayam, encouraged me with his insights and allowed me to use the Department Library. Thanks are due to him too! My teachers, Dr. Kiran Sebastian, Dr. Sathi Clarke at UTC, Bangalore, and Dr. K. G. Pothen (FFRRC), made helpful comments on some of my papers. Dr. Bas Wielenga, former Professor, TTS, Madurai, taught me to tease out of the scriptures issues of labour.

Thanks are also due to the Library Staff of Orthodox Theological Seminary, Kottayam; Mar Thoma Theological Seminary, Kottayam; Kerala United Theological Seminary, Kottayam; Tamil Nadu Theological Seminary, Madurai; United Theological College, Bangalore; Pontifical Seminary, Vadavathoor, Kottayam; Department of International Relations and Politics, M. G. University, Kottayam; and the University Library, M. G. University, Kottayam.

I am also grateful to Rev. Dr. Ashish Amos, General Secretary, ISPCK, for publishing this book.

Foreword

The book, *Child Labour in India: Challenges for Theological Thinking and Christian Ministry in India*, aims to stir the reader out of his or her adult Christianity, adult conceptualisations, adult complacency and adult concerns. In general, children matter in society; their position and role in society have to be given due space and recognition. In particular, children forced or enticed into labour need solidarity and empowerment in their struggles for a life of dignity, rights and fulfillment. Jesus himself eagerly invites children in his life, "Let the little children come to me and do not stop them; for it is to such as these that the kingdom of God belongs" (Mark.10:14; Luke. 20:28; cf. Matt. 19:14).

The rights of children contained in the United Nations Convention on the Rights of the Child can be classified, as Rohan points out, into four broad categories: Subsistence Rights, which contain the rights to food, shelter and health care; Development Rights, which allow children to reach their fullest potential, including education and freedom of thought, conscience and religion; Protection Rights, such as the right to life and to protection from abuse, neglect or exploitation; and Participation Rights, which give space to children to take an active role in community and political life.

The above-mentioned rights remain a utopian dream for children forced or enticed into labour. Rohan observes that children are commoditised as subservient identities for lesser wages; they are deprived of the joys and rights of childhood and made to go through the gruesome grind of inhuman working routines and conditions. Their non-resilient nature and inability to rebel against injustice are abused for the sake of profit. Labouring girl-children, in particular, are subject to greater sexual abuse. Adults, as they do not experience the suffering of such children, may not be able to fully understand the plight of child labourers and so cannot comprehensively represent the predicament of child labour. While this does not take away from adults the obligation to voice out the plight of children, such responsibilities should not turn into patronising acts.

Class, caste, gender, ethnicity and globalisation are the main factors that contribute to the plight of workers and the marginalised, especially children, in the 'unorganised' sector. Therefore, the hermeneutical task of interpreting the labouring circumstances of children in the light of scriptures and liberative narratives is of paramount importance. Rohan's study attempts to move beyond the 'adults only' frame of mind and shows how living with child labour basically takes the shape of a dialogue in which the growing spheres of adults and children are collaborated in an eternal theological conversation. The dynamics include the unrelenting influence of children over the adult experience of God and the values of God's reign in society.

Children should be seen as 'persons' and given their due place as full members of religious communities and society. The deprived childhood of these labourers, their crushed innocence, their throttling environment and deprived identity and their dreams and aspirations should constitute the resources for a liberative theology and an empowering Christian ministry among them.

Rev. Dr. Roger Gaikwad

Preface

In India today, one of the crucial concerns is the unsettled childhood and displaced identity of child labourers. Recent researches and reports on child labour show that most of the labourers are from Dalit and other backward castes, exposing the caste-class nexus perpetuated subtly and overtly to date. A considerable number of girl-children in labour force adds the gender dimension to the nexus. It is only timely to mention that the pathetic state of child labourers has been too unique and too important to be unattended to in our theological discourses. This hermeneutical overlooking has the child labourers not being considered as specific theological category where their unique plight and desires could be assessed and addressed. Therefore, when the majority of the labouring children is from the marginalised communities, an inquiry into their plight is demanding, and more suitably through a critique of different forms of Indian Christian thought, especially the Indian forms of liberation theology.

Theological thinking in India has been, yet unhurriedly, accommodating into its theological discourse many of the unique debates about the problem of child labour. Interestingly, a majority of the child labourers belong to Dalit communities and other marginalised castes and tribes who form the majority of the Christian population in India. Indian Christian Theology, in general, and liberation theology, in particular, have so far focused mainly on the oppressed religious, socio-political, cultural and economic history of the adults, and have pointed out that the life situation of the labouring children of their communities is similar to that of the adults. The repercussion is the over-sighting of the unique oppressive situation of child labourers in the theological and hermeneutical articulations in India.

The forgetfulness on the part of theology about children has emerged from the mindset that children are insignificant beings until they are adults. This can be witnessed both in State policies and in religious and liturgical activities. In the State, children are secondary citizens and not adult enough to be considered or consulted. Their unrepresented state has also meant that their still small voices are not enough represented by adults. The thus depowered children are taken advantage of and silenced at any possible attempt to express their grievances in their own style. The United Nations Convention on Child Rights (1989) has brought back the focus on children while this should have been taken up as issues of Human Rights. Therefore, UNCRC is both complementary and resistive to the biased notion of human rights. The plight of children is not much different in our churches. In many prominent Christian traditions, they are half-members since their baptism or dedication, and attain 'full' membership only after their confirmation or adult-baptism. Theologically, they are treated as not matured enough to comprehend God's grace and sacramental practices of the Church while they are quickly tagged with the "original sin." As many children have expressed, children are starved at the Lord's Table. Critically presenting the same, all our activities, either in the Church or in the State, are child-unfriendly, too "logically" and "rationally" designed and structured, which keep children away. This has left our churches and theologies impoverished by the much significant, 'small' voices of children. Our theological communities have failed to be the much-required monitoring agencies for vulnerable children.

Need for Giving Thought to Child Labour

To a large extent, our theological stances on child-related issues have propelled the way we have been doing missions. Here are some of the typical notions about children:

- Childhood is a stage that every one should grow out of because childhood is an insignificant stage

- Adulthood is the epitome of maturity and wisdom, so children should look up to adults as ultimate models

- More critically, childhood is to be taken advantage of, to lead a child to greater knowledge ("pedagogy")

- Theologically, children do not reflect a complete image of God as God is an adult

- Because children are not complete images of God, they cannot be full members of the body of Christ. Therefore, they could be kept away from sacraments, liturgical celebrations and other decision-making activities of the Church.

Theological reflections about child labour advocate compelling reasons for liberation and meaningful childhood of child labourers. Firstly, it substantiates in theological terms the presence and identity of labouring children, not only to highlight their presence, but also to strive towards their emancipation. In other words, it puts child labourers in the centre of theological discourse and provides a lens through which theological themes traded hitherto could be "reconfigured." Secondly, it further traces exploitative mechanisms that tarnish and destroy God's image in and dignity of the children and engages in deliberations with fellow beings to heighten the awareness and to organise into a meaningful praxis. While explaining the discordant facts of child labour until the state of their emancipation and further, one encounters blockades to God's gracious vision for labouring children. Therefore, a theology to this effect is to liberate the child from the labour force. Biblical insights inform us that such a theology has the task of embracing the influential and potential religious significance of children and the cultural milieu that these significances operate in.

In the process, theological formulations and hermeneutical tools are to be advanced with an eye on bringing the participation of child labourers within the hermeneutical sphere so that their plight is known in their own words. It is here that theology in India broadens its scope by involving child-labour issues.

By critically investigating the problems of child labourers, this work attempts to fulfill the following objectives:

- It highlights the need for more serious theological reflections on the place of children in Christian thought by reflecting on its current attitude towards and assumptions about childhood. This means to overcome the culture of child de-valuation, commodification and neglect. It stresses the urgent need for comprehensive theological reflections on the topic of labour from the perspective of child labour, particularly considering new contexts of globalisation and neo-colonialism.

- It reveals the limitations of the present hermeneutical tools to address these needs of child labour. It promotes the concerns of child labour as a special theological category demanding special attention to children as the bearers of Image of God and emphasising their representation, identity and right to express their marginalised position.

This work critically draws insights from postcolonial criticism and theology along with the method of advocacy to appraise the extent to which Christian Theology, especially Liberation Theolgoy in India, has not realised the liberation as far as child labourers are concerned. Here, the methodological insights are employed as "an interventionist instrument." This appraises the colonised people highlighting their culturally and psychologically colonised state, the effects of colonisation and colonial ideals on people's personalities, the possibilities of reconstructing new identities and the dubiousness of not only the colonial past, but also the contemporary world order in the form of globalisation and its neo-colonising tendencies.

This methodology facilitates in:

- Delving deeper into the factors behind the mask of "poverty" as the cause of child labour and interrogating the totalising tendencies of caste-class-gender merger and the related dynamics, such as power politics, gender politics and identity politics, as primary contributors to child labour. It also evaluates the colonial hangover explicit in the legislations on child labour.

- It critically appraises liberation theology as liberative in nature, but disallows it as having attained an inclusive emancipatory stance for marginalised communities. In this light, it tries to examine specifically how child labourers from marginalised castes are hermeneutically overlooked in liberation theological discourses. This leads to see how child labourers could be an equally important theological category within the broader framework of liberation theology. It is achieved at the theoretical level and facilitates child labourers to boldly and engagingly voice their disagreement.

The advantage of postcolonial criticism is that it is interdisciplinary in nature. It produces intersections or "in-between space" by critically cutting through hegemonic schemes. These spaces give rise to neglected identities and establish them as definitionally crucial. In this work, postcolonial criticism assists the neglected presence and voices of labouring children in our theological thinking and ministry by critiquing the influence of modernity and capitalism on our theologies, especially liberation theology in India. These thoughts are chapterized thus: Chapter 1 focuses on the intricacies involved in addressing the issues of child labour in India. It looks into how these debates are mainly centred on the issues of caste, class, gender and neoliberalisation and how these power struggles have created a pathetic gap between the real-life situation of labouring children and their liberation. In Chapter 2, the focus is on discerning varieties of positions that the Bible and our theologies take about children and labour and how we could retrieve many of the marginalised liberative traditions in these discourses. These liberative discourses provide Chapter 3 with guidelines to engage in theological conversations to delineate hermeneutical keys for the liberation of our theologies from their adult-modes to accept the experiences of child labourers as a starting point of theologising.

Rohan Gideon

Introduction

The National Council of Churches in India is pleased to announce the publication of this work *Child Labour in India: Challenges for Theological Thinking and Christian Ministry in India* by Rev. Rohan Gideon. For the last hundred years since its inception, the NCCI has played a pioneering role in identifying key issues that have challenged the church and society in India. By doing so, it has invested its resources in capacity building, promoting theological thinking and plunging into grass roots concerns and movements for tangible just change. Therefore, this work is a contribution to that illustrious tradition. NCCI's Campaign for Child Rights is an integral part of the core of its theological vision, and its commitment to 'Just Theology'. The Commission for Justice, Peace and Creation is happy to publish this book as part of this Campaign.

This commitment and perspective is timely. According to UNICEF, the child mortality rate in India is about 1.83 million per year—the highest in the world. In 2009, at the world level, child mortality aggregate was 8.1 million. As per the statistical report of WHO, around 1,000 children—below the age of 5—die every hour. UNICEF goes on to say that around 70 per cent of incidents of global child morality happen in developing countries, of which 66 per cent are preventable. They are preventable because they are caused by malnutrition, malaria and acute respiratory infections, problems which could be easily done away with if society was responsible. Several hundred female children die in their mother's womb: the womb of mothers become tombs of these babes. They do not see the light of day. Several hundred innocent children are either infected or affected by HIV/AIDS and die at a young age. The world loses several generations, because they are not rescued from the clutches of untimely death. Of those who survive, the childhood of many comes with a heavy price: the cost of childhood itself. Young girls are raped to satisfy human lust and even killed by brutal men. Then again, several million children are forced to migrate to different places as child labourers, sex and tour escorts, etc., and are exploited.

A world without children is unimaginable. At the same time, a world with children at risk should be equally unimaginable.

Is it not untimely response that costs the lives of many potential messiahs of our time? Yes, it is! Would the birth of children today challenge some of the traditional notions of our society? Yes it would, if we patiently listen to the voices of the lowly from this 'marginal' community of children. They come as prophetic voices if they are discerned.

This book comes with a call to discern such voices in the articulation of our theologies and in the living out of our spiritualities. Children's own voices and the agential significance of these voices will take our theologies and ethics and ethos to near completion. To this effect, we present this work to our esteemed readers and partners in our ecumenical journey.

<table>
<tr><td>A. Samuel Jeyakumar</td><td>R. Christopher Rajkumar</td></tr>
<tr><td>Chairperson</td><td>Executive Secretary</td></tr>
</table>

Commission on Justice, Peace and Creation
Lent 2011

Abbreviations

ABD	Anchor Bible Dictionary
AJT	Asian Journal of Theology
AJTR	Arasaradi Journal of Theological Review
CACL	Campaign Against Child Labour
CRC	Child Rights Convention
DNTB	Dictionary of New Testament Background
ECFW	Encyclopedia of Child and Family Welfare
EPW	Economic and Political Weekly
ER	Ecumenical Review
GJTS	Gurukul Journal of Theological Studies
HTR	Harvard Theological Review
ILO	International Labour Organization
JAAR	Journal of the American Academy of Religion
JBL	Journal of Biblical Literature
JPT	Journal of Pastoral Theology
JR	The Journal of Religion
JSNT	Journal for the Study of New Testament

JSS	Journal for Social Sciences
JSSR	Journal for the Scientific Study of Religion
MCE	The Modern Catholic Encyclopedia
NIDNTT	New International Dictionary of New Testament Theology
NIDOTTE	The New International Dictionary of Old Testament Theology and Exegesis
NPNF	A Select Library of Nicene and Post-Nicene Fathers
NRSV	New Revised Standard Version
RS	Religion and Society
SA	Social Action
ThT	Theology Today
UNICEF	United Nations International Children Educational Fund
WBC	Word Biblical Commentary

CHAPTER 1

Child Labour Debates and Power Dynamics

It is common knowledge that India has the largest number of child labourers in the world.[1] As if this was not unsettling enough, the deliberations on child labour, being situated at the intersections of economic, cultural, legal, religious and social institutions, have eluded attempts to comprehend, address and confront the phenomenon of child labour. While any discrimination based on caste, class, gender and tribe is "racial",[2] traditionally, a strong caste-class enterprise has been, and continues to be, the bedrock for child labour in India. This chapter examines the serious fallouts of such a nexus and their collaboration with other institutions like neocolonisation in the

---

[1] Avtar Singh, "Child Labour Problems and Prospects: Socio-Legal Measures," *SA* 54/4 (Oct-Dec), 396-97. Most of the literature on Child Labour, especially of Child Labour in India, attest to this fact.

[2] Centre for Concern for Child Labour: *A Statement submitted to the National Committee set up by the Prime Minister of India (facilitated by the UNE Division of the Ministry of External Affairs Government of India) in preparation for the World Conference against Racism held in Durban, South Africa, in September 2001. http://www.crin.org/docs/resources/publications/ cccl.pdf.* (9 Nov. 2007) For similar views, see, Manoranjan Mohanty, *Caste, Class, Gender...*, 36.

form of globalisation. These collaborations are perceived not only as the determinants of the economic activity like child labour, but also as the ones "producing and circulating meanings" about and identities of the labouring children. Another intriguing challenge is to comprehend and evaluate the sector that child labour conceptually comes under: the unorganised sector or the informal sector.[3] Prakash Louis observes that being in the workforce of the unorganised sector is not only an economic reality, but also a social and political reality in the Indian context. Most of the workers of

---

[3] The unorganised sector/informal sector includes home-based work, self-employed work, piece wage (sometimes in kind), time wage work, etc. While it provides opportunity for employment creation, production and income generation, it, nevertheless, is characterised by small size temporary and instable operations, labour-intensive technique, unregulated and high competition product market, low levels of earnings, skills acquired through working, more chances of exploitation due to non-existence of trade unions, and no government support. The features that characterised unorganised work include lack of regulation of employment, seasonality of employment, denial of benefits under the labour laws, lack of social security protection and the absence of an employer-employee relationship. The reasons to so "unorganise" the labour may be of economic recession, evasion of tax as well as excessive governmental regulation of the market sector. In contrast, the organised sector is defined as all public sector establishments employing ten or more workers. It is protected by structured labour laws that promise security of job, wages, incentives, health care and related services, education, housing, post-retirement benefits, etc. There is less chance of exploitation of labour due to the existence of trade union. It has official spokespersons and has access to government favours. The two sectors are, however, not separated from each other. For a comparative analysis of these sectors and their working in different states of India, see Siddhartha Sarkar, "Theorizing in Informal Sector: Concept and Context", *SA* 54/4 (Oct-Dec 2004): 359-373; Supriya Roy Chowdhury, "Globalization and Labour", *Economic and Political EPW* 39/4 (Jan. 3 2004), 105; NCC Review CXXVII/ 7 (Aug. 2007), under the theme: 'Labour and Life in India'.

Prakash Louis, "Editorial," *SA* 54/4 (Oct-Dec), iv- v. This issue of *Social Action* has been dedicated to discuss the challenges thrown up in unorganised sectors.

the informal sector come from the Dalit, tribal minority and the most marginalised caste communities. It is this reality that escapes many social scientists who examine this phenomenon. Caste, class, ethnicity and gender are fundamentally contributive factors to being a worker in the unorganised sector. Since the ruling elite comes from the dominant communities, it has no political will to address these issues. The rural-urban bias is another factor one has to observe in this sector.

Scholars have made efforts to decipher this web of determinants and lay these concerns threadbare with mixed results. This chapter analyses these concerns and sees how terms like "child", "child labour", "child rights" and the related emancipatory discourses have been dealt with and articulated by policy-making bodies and experts at the conceptual level and at the level of implementation in a neo-colonial milieu. United Nations Convention for Rights of Children (UNCRC) will serve as a broader framework. UNCRC elaborates rights based on non-discrimination; devotion to the best interest of the child; the right to life, survival and development; and respect for the views of the child. It covers the full spectrum of civil, political, economic, social and cultural rights, stressing their indivisible and interdependent relationships. It presents with clarity how children have the right to be heard and to have their own opinions on matters affecting them taken into account, agreeing with their age and wisdom.

Defining *Child* and *Labour*

Theoretically, definitions are designed with presumed solutions or a hypothesis that one has for a problem. In our case, child labour as a peculiar challenge, refers to the employment of children in gainful occupation, something that is hateful and exploitative,[4] and that which impairs the development and well-being of children. Homer Folk, former Chairperson of US Child Labour

---

[4] Avtar Singh, "Child Labour Problems and Prospects,"…, 396-97

Commission, defined child labour as "any work by children that interferes with their full physical development and their opportunities for a desirable minimum level of education or their needed recreation."[5] In a less subjective sense, a child is a "labourer" if she or he is "economically active."[6] According to ILO, "Child labour includes children permanently leading adult lives, working long hours for low wages under conditions damaging to their health and to their physical and mental development, sometimes separated from their families, frequently deprived of meaningful educational and training opportunities that could open up for them a better future."[7] These forms of labour generally remain "unskilled," underpaid and underprivileged throughout and restrict the labourer's physical and mental health. According to United Nations' System of National Accounts (SNA), the production of economic goods and services includes wage employment, self- employment and participation in agriculture, milling, handicrafts, construction and water and wood collection.[8]

Defining "child labour" is a task in itself, as it involves deliberations on tapestried issues like "child," "labour," "work" and "childhood." These deliberations are again taken up with "adulthood" and multi-cultural discourses as reference points. These terms and concepts are unique to each cultural and political milieu. Therefore, their imposing subjectivity or their ruthless

---

[5] Avtar Singh, "Child Labour Problems and Prospects,"..., 397

[6] Quoted from Kebebew Ashagrie's "Statistics on Child Labour," in *Bulletin of Labour Statistics* No. 3 (1993) by Kaushik Basu, *Child Labour: Cause, Consequence and Cure, with Remarks on International Labour Standards, 6, http://www.essex.ac.uk/armedcon/story_id/000413.pdf* (9 Nov. 2007)

[7] Avtar Singh, "Child Labour Problems and Prospects,"..., 397

[8] Eric V. Edmonds, *Child Labour, http://www.dartmouth.edu/per cent7Eeedmonds/clhbk.pdf* (9 Nov. 2007)

technicality has created umpteen discourses on the identity, freedom and opportunities of children. Definitions and their trajectories provided by United Nations Convention on Rights of Children (UNCRC), International Labour Organistion (ILO) and the definitions worked out in our own country would be the starting points for our discussion.

ILO has charted out some "worst forms of labor," which include forced involvement of children in prostitution and production of pornography. A quick look at the list widens the scope of our understanding of the gravity of the ills of child labour. In 1999, the 184 member nations of ILO passed the Worst Forms of Child Labour Convention (Convention 182). Article 3 of Convention 182 defines "worst forms" as:

- All forms of slavery or practices similar to slavery, such as the sale and trafficking of children, debt bondage and serfdom and forced or compulsory labour, including forced or compulsory recruitment of children for use in armed conflict;

- The use, procuring or offering of a child for prostitution, for the production of pornography or for pornographic performances;

- The use, procuring or offering of a child for illicit activities, in particular for the production and trafficking of drugs as defined in the relevant international treaties; work, which, by its nature or the circumstances in which it is carried out, is likely to harm the health, safety or morals of children.[9]

There are conflicting definitions of "child labour" based on age. Debating on the basis of the age of the labourer, United Nations Convention on the Rights of the Child defines a "child" as anyone

---

[9] *Worst Forms of Child Labour Convention, 1999 (No. 182): http:// www.ohchr.org/english/law/childlabour.htm* (Children's Day 2007).

up to the age of 18 and categorically forbids the employment and exploitation of children.[10] If the scheme of compulsory education is any reference, the least possible age of employment is the minimum age of completion of mandatory schooling. Biological categories too become important factors in determining a "child." Adding to the debate, National Commission for Enterprise in the Unorganised Sector sets 10 to 14 as the age group for defining "child labour."[11] However, it is common sense that these numbers only lobby to have more children into the labour force than not. The debates should also consider the climatic conditions and other factors; children at different geographical set-ups attain puberty at different ages. In the societal valorisation of "adult" and "children" and semi-feudal relationship in agrarian setups, our legal laws and cultural practices have not given children adequate constitutional protection through proper definition.

On the notions of "work" and "labour," there is a tendency to differentiate "work" from "labour." "Work" is treated as a positive move towards socialising children into the thought patterns and working patterns of a community, while "'labour" is perceived as exploitative. Deliberations on "work" and/or "labour" would hardly make a difference as long as children are not privileged with the needs and care of childhood.

The ILO often distinguishes between "child work" and "child labor," the latter being used to describe the more pejorative part of "child work," whereas "child work" in itself could include doing light household chores and can actually have some learning value (ILO, 1995). Recent ILO estimates suggest that "child labor" is

---

[10] *The Constitution of India and Child Labour* (Mysore: CACL, 2003), 5. (Henceforth "Mysore Document").

[11] National Commission for Enterprise in the Unorganised Sector "The Challenge of Employment in India : An Informal Economy Perspective: Vol. 1- Main Report", *http://nceus.gov.in/The Challenge of Employment in India.pdf* (May 5, 2010), 47.

taken to include those who do part-time work. Some economists adopt the convention of distinguishing between "work" and "home care," classifying children who do not attend school and are not formally employed as "home care labourers."[12] Practically observed, child labour, though always synonymous with market work, makes the case for the lives of children involved in labour. Reviewing child labour by giving it a human face can help in approaching this problem in a wholistic manner, as this research intends.

A Critical Review of the Situation of Child Labour in India

Historically, the traditional Indian society has been the fertile ground for child labour. The orientation for children to labour in India could be traced back to theories of socialisation, a preoccupation with population growth and unfair economic competition. Children were directed to participate in household help, family occupation especially in agriculture and other business where no special skills were required. Neel Sharda traces the history of such labour back to Kautilya's *Arthashastra*, which mentions that children below eight years of age worked in the households of nobles. In medieval times, children were engaged as trainees under artisans and craftspeople, where on the pretext for training, children were not given their due remuneration. Even in the bonded labour system, where a male adult was employed by a landowner, his entire family, including the children, was engaged.[13] There have been times when such types of participation were treated as unpleasant to the child, but desirable, somewhat

---

[12] Kaushik Basu, Child Labour: Cause, Consequence and Cure, with Remarks on International Labour Standards, *http://www.essex.ac.uk/armedcon/story id/000413*.pdf (9. 11. 2007).

[13] Neel K. Sharda, *The Legal, Economic and Social Status of the Indian Child* (New Delhi: National Book Organisation, 1988), 21- 22. For a greater detail of this reading, see J. C. Kulshreshta, *Child Labour in India* (New Delhi: Ashish Publishing House, 1978), 48- 49.

akin to our contemporary view of education or socialisation. While on one hand, work as a direct fulfillment of a child's natural abilities and creative potentialities is always conducive to a healthy growth, work enforced as means of overcoming economic constraints of a family, or a community or a society becomes enslaving in character and deleterious in its impact.[14]

Types of Child Labour in India

Technically, child labour, as an unorganised form of labour, can be classified into four categories based on the nature of work. They are:

- Home-based work
- Self-employed
- Piece Wage work
- Time Wage work

Working sectors in rural areas include fields, plantations, domestic help, forestry, fishing and cottage industry, while urban types include domestic help, shops, restaurants, small and large industries, transport, communication and jobs like newspaper and milk distribution, shoe-shining, rag-picking, rickshaw-pulling, having sex for money, fighting and carrying people's bags and other loads. Generally, child labourers are engaged in:

- Cultivation and agriculture
- Livestock, forestry, fishing, hunting, plantation and orchard
- Mining and quarrying
- Manufacturing, servicing, processing and repair
- Construction
- Trade and commerce

---

[14] Kaushik Basu, *http://www.essex.ac.uk/armedcon/story id/000413.pdf* (9. 11. 2007)

- Transport, storage and communication
- Other services[15]

Statistical Analysis: Some Insights

Data available for the last 30 to 40 years depict either a regrettable rise or *status quo* in the percentage of child labourers in India. Moreover, the data projected by the Government of India (2-20 million) drastically contradict those as estimated by ILO ("the incidence of child labour grows at an annual rate of 4 per cent"), UNICEF ("10-40 million in India in 1997") and Commission on Labour Standards and International Trade.[16] According to the 1991 census, India has a child population (0-14 years) of 197 millions, of which 12.7 million are full-time child workers and about 10.6 million are marginal child workers. Between 1999 and 2003, UNICEF investigated that in India, 14 per cent of children (5-14 years) are in child labour. Among them, 14 per cent are male children (5-14 years) and 15 per cent female children (5-14 years).[17] Any depiction of decline in the ratio as presented by the Government is insignificantly marginal without altering any of the tapestried issues. As observed in the previous section, rural areas have contributed greatly to the child-labour data.

The period between 1971 and 1986 has seen an increase in the number of child labourers in correspondence with the rise in the population, with a great majority of the labourers engaged in the

---

[15] *ECFW*, edited by Laxmi Devi, vol. 4 [Child Labour] (Lucknow/ New Delhi: Institute for Sustainable Development/ Anmol Publications Pvt. Ltd., 1998), 140- 141.

[16] Geeta Chowdhry, "Postcolonial Interrogations of Child Labour", in *Power, Postcolonialism and International Relations: Reading Race, Gender and Class*, edited by Geeta Chowdhry and Sheila Nair, 1st Indian Reprint, (London and New York: Routledge, 2003), 225

[17] UNICEF, *India—Child Labour, http://www.unicef.org/infobycountry/ india statistics.html1* (Children's Day 2007).

agricultural set-up in rural areas.[18] The agricultural sector—known as the "hidden" sector for child labour—employed 76 per cent of child labour in 1991. The percentage of child labour involved in the manufacturing sector rose from 3.1 per cent of total child labour in 1971 to 5.7 per cent in 1991.[19] Approaching the issue from the viewpoint of school dropouts, the data suggests that the identity and whereabouts of nearly 57 million neither account as child labourers nor school-going. The State seems to take the definition of "child labour" only in letter, not in spirit: the lives of 57 million children are unaccounted for.[20]

Equally significant for our consideration is the report of the National Commission for Enterprise in the Unorganised Sector (NCEUS). In its broader picture of the year 2007, the Commission's report on "Conditions of Work and Promotion of Livelihoods in Unorganised Sector" has exposed the "utterly deplorable" conditions with "extremely few livelihood options" of the workers in this sector. Around 86 per cent of the labour force in India belongs to this sector, and around 77 per cent had an income below Rs. 20 a day. An interesting observation of this report is that 88 per cent of the Schedule Tribes and Schedule Castes, 80 per cent of the Other Backward Castes and 85 per cent of Muslims

---

[18] In 1971, it was 10.7 million (93per cent in rural area), in 1981, 14. 5 million, in 1983 it was 17.4 million (90 per cent in rural India) and, in 1986 it was 110 million (87per cent from rural area). Neel K. Sharda, *The Legal, Economic and Social Status...*, 54-55.

[19] Kaushik Basu, *http://www.essex.ac.uk/armedcon/story_id/000413.pdf* (9.11.2007). Also, note that out of the 12.7 million full-time child labourers, 35.2 per cent worked as cultivators while 42.5per cent were agricultural labourers. It is also estimated that there were 2.6 million bonded labourers, of which at least 8per cent were children. Vasanthi Raman, *Globalisation and Child Labour, http://www.revolutionarydemocracy.org/ rdv4n1/childlab.htm* (Children's Day, 2007).

[20] Shantha Sinha, "Child Labour and Education," *Seminar* 474 (February 1994), 14-15.

belong to this sector. "Most Unorganised Workers get below Rs. 20 a day."[21] This gives a clear picture of the social groups that continue to contribute physically to the dehumanising labour force. This deplorable condition has forced younger family members to work for the survival of their families. In its latest observation, the commission has sharpened its focus on the age group and observes the presence of nearly 7per cent children below 14 years of age in the above-mentioned labour force, while the presence of children between the ages of 15 and 19 is a glaring 39 per cent.[22]

Here, two dynamics should be noted. Firstly, the glaring difference between the percentage of children in the labour force between two cut-off age-groups, i.e., 14 years and 19 years, shows the hurriedness of exploitative forces to push children to labour force once they have reached a legally safe age of 15. While it is 7 per cent below 14 years, it is a pole-apart 39 per cent between 15 and 19 years. Secondly, this analysis confirms the view on how children from most marginalised communities are forced into the labour sector and deprived of the basic rights of compulsory education and healthy and playful childhood. These facts make it imperative for our theologies to take up the issues of child labour with unreserved commitment and absolute seriousness.

Caste-Class-Gender-Neocolonisation Nexus in Child Labour Discourses

Why children work? This question has evoked responses from the perspectives that researchers have taken. While the following determinants are presented under "separate" debates, they are a tapestried lot.

---

[21] *The Hindu* (Kochi, 10 Aug. 2007), 14.

[22] National Commission for Enterprise in the Unorganised Sector,... 48.

The Poverty Debate

This debate supports the inevitability of child labour that has to be reckoned with. Experts like Neel Sharda, K. K. Khatu, Sabita Babani and others[23] subscribe to the view that extreme poverty is the main determinant of child labour in India. Agriculture as the main occupation of the majority of the population is another premise on which this debate persists. It is also argued that child labour is very cheap and readily available in agricultural and rural sectors—both in primary and secondary jobs.[24] Poverty makes parents prioritise working to schooling. In such serious cases, age restrictions and other safety measures are compromised with. Otherwise, the belief is that children would turn into anti-social elements by resorting to thieving and similar income-oriented activities.

Kaushik Basu and Pham Hoang Van show that "child labour as a mass phenomenon occurs not because of parental selfishness but because of the parents' concern for the household's survival." Basu and Van establish that "a family will send the children to the labour market only if the family's income from non-child-labour sources drops very low." This is why, they stated, "the children of the non-poor seldom work even in very poor countries... In other words, children's leisure or, more precisely, non-work is a luxury good in the household's consumption in the sense that a poor household cannot afford to consume this good, but it does so as soon as the household income rises sufficiently."[25]

---

[23] Neel Sharda, *The Legal, Economic and Social Status of the Indian Child*; K. K. Khatu, *The Working Children in India* (Baroda Operation Research Group, 1983); Sabita Babani, "Child Labour: A Social Problem," *The Economic Times* (April 10, 1982); and, Centre of Social Research, *Working Condition of Children Employed in Unorganised Sector- A Case in Sivakasi* (Madras: 1984).

[24] *ECFW*: Also see, Shantha Sinha, "Child Labour and Education,"..., 14-19.

[25] *http://www.indiauncut.com/iublog/article/why-children-labour/* (15 Sep. 2006).

Many cannot afford education although elementary education is free (and however low the other related expenses could be). There is a general perception that uneducated children are an asset and that the desire to educate them becomes "double liability." Gender typing of work makes the situation worse for girls. Girls are found as domestic help and minding their younger siblings. Therefore, the argument goes that "any attempt to abolish... [child labor] through legal recourse would, under the circumstances, not be practical since this would put the already poor families under acute economic stress."[26] However, the other side of the argument is that child labour is all the more justified with concern for the employers than for the children and their families[27] because poverty is a consequence of disproportionate accumulation of beneficial resources, constituted by *en suite* imbalance and a pattern of expansion, which advances these disproportionate features.

The Illiteracy Debate

A commonly understood argument of the families for not sending their children to school is "inadequate schools," "lack of schools," or even "the expense of schooling" and therefore leaving some children with little else to do but work. Nearly 53.95 million children did not attend school during 1999-2000, which would mean 62.35 million children in the labour force, or 27.32 per cent of the child population between 5 and 14 years of age. In India, the 1999-2000 National Sample Survey (NSS) data indicate a high incidence of child labour, with 8.4 million children active in the

---

[26] Shantha Sinha "Child Labour and Education"..., 15-16. Studies conducted show that child Labour in *rural areas* is often 'light', so much so that these children ought to be able to get education without seriously cutting into their work commitments, *if* they had access to proper schools. Kaushik Basu, *http://www.essex.ac.uk/armedcon/story id/ 000413.pdf* (9. 11. 2007)

[27] Shantha Sinha "Child Labour and Education,"..., 16

labour force. If the wider definition of child labour is accepted, which is that all the children who do not attend school should be counted as child labour, the incidence of child labour is enormous.

The attitudes of parents also contribute to child labour; some parents feel that children should work in order to develop skills useful in the job market, instead of taking advantage of formal education.[28] The vicissitudes of rural agricultural and non-agricultural work and the schedule of schools do not necessarily preclude school-going children from working for wages or in family occupations. Schools, which could be a source to wean children out of the labour market and put them through a process of learning and skill-enhancement, would not implement the necessary objectives.

Shanta Sinha argues that if the official sources put the figure of child labour at 17 million and those not attending schools in the 5-14 age-group are nearly 74 million, the government's schemes and legislations on child labour would cater only to those 17 million. Her contention is that these school dropouts are never "idle" but are invariably drawn into various forms of household labour and are deprived of the attention and benefits promised by the schemes and legislations. Therefore, they are "missing" children, and any later legislation would ignore their presence as child labourers.

The Class-Caste Interface Debate

The teasing out of the strands of caste structure and its economic implications related to the social mobility of child labourers in India is largely overlooked by many scholars and researchers because it strikes at the age-old bedrock of the traditional social

---

[28] Azadi India Foundation, *Child Labour in India*, *http://azadindia.org/social-issues/child-labour-in-india.html* (Children's Day, 2007).

structure.[29] The tapestried phenomenon of class-caste is also attributed to the growth of capitalism in India. This has its roots in the British colonial regime where the British made use of the local raw material and, when necessary, labour. Analysing this trend, Manoranjan Mohanty explains[30] how later, in post-independent India, modern technology-based industrialisation rose on the profits of Green Revolution. This happened largely in states like Punjab, Haryana and Uttar Pradesh, and some pockets of other states. A semi-feudal system and poverty persisted in many of these states including Bihar, Madhya Pradesh and Orissa. The labour force in these regions was not only landless and unorganised, but also from scheduled castes, backward classes and scheduled tribes.

The overwhelming majority (around 85 per cent[31]) of child labourers in India comes from communities and groups that are at the lower rungs of our traditional, caste-based social hierarchy, i.e., the SCs, STs, OBCs and minorities, especially Muslims. This

---

[29] Although it's hard to find exact figure of child labourers in terms of percentage - at national level- who are dalits, one can draw this sort of conclusion by putting together data researched at state levels and in various types of child labour units at various levels. The explanation of many such conclusion are as "nearly ninety percent are dalits", "more than ninety percent are dalits" and "almost all are dalits." Even the UNICEF in one of its recent research reports has agreed with this magnanimity of the problem. K, Jamanadas, *Caste System Contributed to Child Labour in India,* http://www.ambedkar.org/research/Caste System Contributed To Child Labour In India.htm. (14 Sep. 2006) Also see Global March Against Child Labour, *World Cup Campaign- Child Labour and Sporting Goods, www.globalmarch.org/campaigns/worldcupcampaign/child labour.php;* (15 Sep. 2006)

[30] Manoranjan Mohanty, *Class, Caste and Gender,* 3rd reprint, (New Delhi, SAGE, 2006), 34.

[31] Cf. Fn 28.

amounts to the majority of the Indian population.[32] These, in short, are the poor of India and it is largely from the families and communities of the poor that child labourers come. It is, therefore, not accidental that studies of many of the industries where there is a substantial presence of child labour—industries like the carpet, match, brassware, glass and bangle, lockmaking, slate and gem-polishing industries and tea plantations—show that the overwhelming majority of the children working in these industries come from Scheduled Castes, Scheduled Tribes, Other Backward Classes and Muslim communities. The match industry in Sivakasi is seen to employ mainly Dalit children, especially girls. Glass manufacturing industry in the Firozabad district has around 45 per cent of its labouring children from SC communities. Among the beedi workers of North Arcot, TN, the majority is from Scheduled Castes and Other Backward Castes. The carpet industry, especially in UP, has 50 per cent hired labour, and a little over 50 per cent of hired help comes from the economically poorer Scheduled Castes and Adivasis.[33]

K. Jamanadas considers caste system as a contributing factor to child labour in India. UNICEF too has made similar studied and researched remarks. Quoting UNICEF, Jamanadas says:

> The rigidity of the caste system in India has, among other things, contributed to the mushrooming of child labour in the country, says the UNICEF. In the report 'The state of the world's children,' the UNICEF said the dominant cultural

---

[32] *ECFW*- vol. 4..., 141. Also see, Manoranjan Mohanty, *Class, Caste, Gender*..., 20.

[33] Geetha B. Nambissan, "Social Exclusion, Children's Work and Education" in *Child Labour and the Right to Education in South Asia: Needs versus Rights*, edited by Naila Kabeer, Geetha B. Nambissan and Ramya Subramanian (New Delhi: Sage Publications, 2003), 115. For similar views, see , Amit Verma, *Why Child Labour? http://www..org/ rdv4n1/childlab.htm* (Children's Day, 2007).

group in India might not wish its own children to do hazardous labour but it would not be so concerned if young people from racial, ethnic or economic minorities did it. Citing the magnitude of child labour, it said, 'In India, the view has been that some people are born to rule and to work with their minds while others, the vast majority, are born to work with their bodies.' 'Many traditionalists had been unperturbed about lower-caste children failing to enroll in or dropping out of school,' the UNICEF said, adding 'and if these children end up doing hazardous labour, it is likely to be seen as their lot in life.' The UNICEF's observation came against the backdrop of the recent Supreme Court judgment banning child labour in hazardous and non-hazardous industries.[34]

Children from marginalised castes and tribes continue to be "structurally disadvantaged" despite amendments to the labour laws and to the issues of caste discrimination in India.

The Class-Caste-Gender-Interface Debate

It is estimated that about one-third of all child labourers in India is girls. Interestingly, in most of the studies, female child labourers are an invisible part of child labour statistics. It is investigated[35] that the interaction of caste-class structures with male-dominant ideologies is one of the main causes contributing to the growing menace of female child labour and the nature of suffering they undergo. In this plight, their biological categories are translated

---

[34] K. Jamanadas, *http://www.ambedkar.org/research/Caste System Contributed To Child Labour In India.htm.*

[35] For a helpful explanation on this reality and for further leads *see* Godwin Shiri and Rohan Gideon, *"The Plight of Female Child Labourers: A Case Study of Workers in Bangalore"*, Religion and Society, Vol. 49/50 (Dec 2004-March 2005), 33-71 [co-authorship clarified in Religion and Society 50/3 (Sep 2005) vi.]. For a detailed treatment of this subject, *see* Peter Robb, "Introduction: Meanings of Labour in Indian Social Context," in *Dalit Movements and the Meanings of Labour in India*, edited by Peter Robb (Delhi: Oxford University Press, 1993), 1-67

into social roles, which have denied these girl-children justice and dignity.

There are specific areas of work where girl-children are preferred to adults and male children. For example, domestic help is an area where the traditional understanding of gender-typing works. Reports suggest "feminisation" of agricultural sector.[36] The traditional treatment of male children as the perpetuators of family tradition has attached more economic value to them, and therefore releases them from works that are traditionally allotted to girl-children. This has disadvantaged girl-children in parental care, where girl-children are paid lesser attention than their male siblings, and perpetuated the dominant ideology. The fact that a majority of domestic help consists of women and girl-children attests to this view.

One of the most unfortunate discriminations that girl-children undergo more often than their male counterparts is sexual abuse. All information on such abuses would not see the light of day as victims either hesitate to share such experiences for the fear of social condemnation, or—as with a younger age group—their inability to comprehend the existence or seriousness of such abuse and lack of awareness of the forms they are expressed in. [37] NCEUS reiterates this in its report by mentioning that in the age group of 10-14, the participation of female children is 7.36 as compared to 7.04 males, especially in rural areas. The same is true for the age group of 5-9.[38]

---

[36] *The Hindu*, Kochi (10 Aug. 2007), 14.

[37] Godwin Shiri and Rohan Gideon, "*The Plight of Female Child Labourers...*, 32- 36.

[38] National Commission for Enterprise in the Unorganised Sector... 66.

The Globalisation Debate

It is plausible that globalisation contributes positively to the lifestyle and technology of the society and possibilities and generates income for economically backward families.[39] However, the real-life situation is far from such notions. One also needs to face the truth of the discomforts that globalisation has brought about. Joseph Stiglitz says that while globalisation has the potential to empower weaker economies, the way it has been managed so far by the leading monetary agencies and trade agreement needs radical rethinking.[40] Dislocation of livelihood under the New Economic Policy as attributed to globalisation is often, in a positive sense, considered as "structural adjustment with a human face."[41] However, the "hollowness of the approach underlying the trickle-down theory gets easily exposed if its implications are laid bare."[42]

The current discussions on child rights and child labour are taking place in this particular international context, i.e., the context of globalisation. Needless to say, the International Monetary Fund and World Bank, as part of a package deal for bailing them out of the debt crisis, have forced structural adjustment programmes on developing nations. A consequential integral element in the

---

[39] Eric V. Edmonds, *http://www.dartmouth.edu/per cent7Eeedmonds/clhbk.pdf* (9 Nov. 2007).

[40] Joseph Stiglitz, *Globalization and Its Discontents*, (New Delhi: Penguin, 2002).

[41] Supriya Roy Chowdhury, "Globalization and Labour"..., 105; Nanjunda D. C. and M. Annapurna, "Small Hands in Silicon City-Bangalore: Some Facts and Experiences at Grass Root Level," *JSS* 13/2, 151: *http://www.krepublishers.com/02-Journals/JSS/JSS-13-0-000-000-2006-Web/JSS-13-2-000-000-2006-Abst-Text/JSS-13-2-151-156-2006-417-Nanjunda-D-C/JSS-13-2-151-156-2006-417-Nanjunda-D-C-Text.pdf* (15 Sep. 2007).

[42] S. P. Shukla, "Globalisation: Lives and Livelihood," a lecture delivered at the National Seminar on *Globalization- Life and Livelihood Issues*, held at Kottayam, Kerala, 28 Feb.- 2 March, 2008.

neo-liberal paradigm is that growth is crucial and that this growth will slowly trickle down to the poor in the long run. As one can notice:

> The process of liberalization and globalization isolate the non-economic considerations from the focal economic considerations of growth and profit. Therefore, the problems of the poor and the deprived may actually get accentuated.[43]

But these are further exacerbated by the operation of the international system wherein developing countries are dependent in myriad ways on industrialised nations. "Colonial inheritance, technical and financial dependence structures and chronically deteriorating terms of trade, and more recently, heavy indebtedness, have contributed and still do contribute very distinctly and very directly to the impoverishment of large sections of Third World populations."[44] In the interaction between the household/family as a micro-economy and economic programmes of the state as a macro-economy ("indigenous capitalism" versus "predatory capitalism"), the pressure on members of family (especially women) to increase family income in the face of inflation and decreasing social sector budgets has resulted in more children being put to work either to substitute for the mother in domestic chores, in the case of girls, or to add to the family kitty.

The interconnectedness of the above determinants can be approached by two large frameworks of thoughts: from the discourse of development, where poverty and related issues like caste-class and globalisation are the key factors, and from the discourse that the educational system is to blame for the unabated

---

[43] Manoranjan Mohanty, *Class, Caste and Gender...*, 23. Also see, Satya Prakash Dash, "Globalization and Labour: The Need for Institutional Mechanism," *Social Action* 58/1 (Jan-March, 2008): 59-72.

[44] Jolly, Richard and Cornia, Andrea Giovanni: "The Impact of World Recession on Children," UNICEF, 1984.

rise in child labour.[45] The legislations and interventions regarding these debates could be sorted out as intra-national, supra-national and extra-national.[46] In the battle against child labor, a variety of laws and legislations have been implemented. The objective of any legislation is to protect the interests of citizens from exploitation. They are the expression of the collective conscience of society and make the functioning conform to this expression.

Conceptual Assessment of the Policies on Child Labour

Constitutional Rights and Legislations on Child Labour

Of late, child labour has drawn considerable policy and public attention. If read and interpreted from the perspective of child labourers, the articles in the Fundamental Rights[47] and Directive

---

[45] For more conceptual explanation of these trends, see Naila Kabeer, "Deprivation, Discrimination and Delivery: Competing Explanations for Child Labour and Educational Failure," in *Child Labour and the Right to Education in South Asia: Needs versus Rights...*, 351- 385.

[46] Intra-national effort consists of the laws that a country enacts and interventions that it plans in order to control child labour within the national boundary. Supra-national interventions are those attempted through international organisations, such as the ILO, the WTO and the UNICEF, which by establishing conventions and encouraging and cajoling nations to ratify them, have tried to curb child labour. The most powerful, and also controversial, instrument that the supra-national institutions can use to curb child labour is the imposition of 'international labour standards', that is, a set of minimal rules and conditions for labour which all countries are expected to satisfy. Since the adoption of such standards makes it possible. Thanks to controversy and a divergence of opinion, the world has been slow to adopt International Labour standards. This has led some developed countries to consider legislation and other action in their own countries, which could curb child labour in developing nations. Such actions are termed extra-national. Kaushik Basu, *http://www.essex.ac.uk/armedcon/story id/ 000413.pdf* (9. 11. 2007).

[47] Articles of Fundamental Rights declare Equality before Law (No. 14), Prohibition of Discrimination (No. 15-3), Protection of Life and Personal Liberty (No. 21), Prohibition of Traffic in Human Beings and Forced Labour (No. 23) and Prohibition of Employment of Children in Factories and other Hazardous Employment (No. 24). "Mysore Document" 1. Also see, *ECFW*, vol. 4..., 22-34.

Principles[48] clearly prohibit employment of children. The Supreme Court of India has held that these fundamental rights be seen not in isolation of each other but as a package of rights to fulfill the mandate outlined in the preamble of our Constitution. Paramount among them is the right to life and to livelihood and the right to live in dignity and security. Employment of children thus violates the essence of Article 21. Article 24 expressly prohibits employment of children in any hazardous work. Although the Constitution does not define "hazardous," for children, it cannot be equated with the same intensity as viewed by able-bodied adults. Even, abiding by the constitutional directives is made mandatory (Article 51). So, employment of children defeats the notion of the holistic development articulated in the Constitution and is, therefore, unconstitutional.

Child labour regulation is an important part of the current debate on international labour standards. The essence of legislation is to safeguard and protect the interests of the people from any form of exploitation and regulate the affairs of society in a satisfactory manner. It is an expression of the collective conscience of society. Up to 1986, fourteen legislative enactments provided legal protection to children in various occupations.[49]

---

[48] From the perspective of labouring children, Directive Principles guide that children of tender age are not abused (No. 39a), that they are given opportunities and facilities to develop in a healthy manner and in conditions of freedom and dignity, and childhood and youth are protected against exploitation and against moral and material abandonment (No. 39f), that they have right to work, to educate and to public assistance in certain areas (No. 41), that they have free and compulsory education (No. 45), that there be promotion of educational and economic interests of Scheduled Castes, Scheduled Tribes and other weaker sections (No. 46), and that the State raise the level of nutrition and the standard of living and improve public health. "Mysore Document"…, 1-2. Also see, *ECFW*, vol. 4…, 22-34.

[49] Factory Act, 1948, Mines Act 1952, Plantation Labour Act 1951, Merchant Shipping Act 1958, Motor Transport Workers Act 1961, Dock Workers Regulation and Employment Act 1948, Children (Pledging of

In all these discourses, one can notice elaborate discussions on the technicalities surrounding the economic issues in the labour market *sans* human face. Geetha Chowdhry contends that comprehending child labour as an economic process also "requires an examination of the production and circulation of commodities as well as meanings".[50]

International Labour Standards in Relation to the Rights of Children

The International Labour Standards as strategic plans are deliberated to help poor countries attain some definite minimal standard of living. As Kaushik Basu detects, poorer nations have suspected an undercover activity of the developed nations in the formulation of the Standards.[51] Intrinsically related to the issues of the Standards are those of Human Rights. It is a paradox that Human Rights apply to full-fledged citizens and children are not sufficiently recognised as full citizens. Shelly Wright explains how women, children and indigenous peoples have usually not been treated as full citizens. Because of this "invisibility," they suffer through inadequate recognition in international economic

---

Labour) Act 1933, Employment of Children Act 1938, Apprentices Act 1961, Beedi and Cigar Works (Condition of Employment) Act 1966, Contract Labour (Regulation and Abolition) Act 1970, Radiation Protection Rules 1971 under the Atomic Energy Act 1962, Shops and Commercial Establishment Acts under different nomenclatures in states, the Juvenile Justice Act 1986. *ECFW-* vol. 4: 58- 72.

[50] Geeta Chowdhry, "Postcolonial Interrogations,"..., 227.

[51] Kaushik Basu, "International Labour Standards and Child Labour," in *Child Labour and the Right to Education in South Asia: Needs versus Rights...*, 95.

policies.[52] Shelley Wright explains the discriminatory approach of the policy-making bodies in defining "human rights" and a "citizen." She says that any unified and potential sovereign subject is the holder of rights. Therefore, either a single person or group-communities (with uniformity of identity) can claim human rights. However, 'abnormality' of gender, age, class, physical and mental "deviants" have been neglected in policy matters. While children contribute to the state economy like any adult, they are deprived of protection by law for various types of violation of rights they undergo. The seriousness of these issues is much deeper. Sheila Nair discusses that Human Rights do not investigate the links between global capital and human rights violations. They are more concerned with the violation of political rights by states and governments.[53] At the conceptual level, Geeta Chowdhry discusses two approaches to human rights. They are (a) the universalist approach and (b) the relativist approach. While the universalist discourse advocates global human rights on the basis of a universal human culture, or one homogenised culture, the Relativists suggest that different histories have offered different cultural

---

[52] See her *International Human Rights, Decolonization and Globalization: Becoming Human* (London: Routledge, 2001), 24- 25, 62, 215, especially Ch. 4, "Subjects, Soldiers and Citizens." Also, see John Wall, "Human Rights in Light of Children: A Christian Childist Perspective," *JPT* 17/ 1 (2007): 54-67. This article argues that Christians should support children's rights and press further for the considerations of children to transform our understanding of human rights as such. Wall says, "Some argue that children lack the full moral autonomy to take on equal rights-holding responsibilities; others that treating children as right-bearing individuals obscures their vulnerabilities and dependency, thus ignoring what makes childhood distinctive; others... see a rights framework as undermining the central importance to children of family responsibilities." 54.

[53] Sheila Nair, "Human Rights and Postcoloniality," in *Power, Postcolonialism and International Relations: Reading Race, Gender and Class...*,256-258.

understandings of rights, which should be globally respected. She comments how both approaches reinstate culture as an entity and a process and homogenise and reify culture. She also notices the role of colonialism in the radicalised and gendered construction of North and South.[54]

Before the 1989 UNCRC's "best interests of the child," the problem of child labour, even in its "worst forms", was seldom addressed as a human rights issue. However, Child Rights activism has brought out the ugly trajectories of child labour. The 1989 Convention streamlines the missing voices that have been representing child labourers' cause and that of the labourers themselves. Very young children rely on others to express their views and protect their best interests;[55] as they grow older, they become more and more able to speak for themselves and to engage in decision-making on their own behalf for their rights.[56] Therefore, UNCRC envisioned a three-pronged rights policy for children: *Protection Rights* (to be protected from maltreatment, neglect and exploitation), *Provision Rights* (access to food, health, education and social security) and *Participation Rights* (to be

---

[54] Geeta Chowdhry, "Postcolonial Interrogations,"..., 229-233.

[55] Maternal Feminism has taken up this cause seriously and suggests asking not only how fresh understanding of children might influence motherhood, but also how contemporary experiences of mothering shape understanding of children. Bonnie J. Miller- McLemore, "'Let the Children Come' Revisited: Contemporary Feminist Theologians on Children" in *The Child in Christian Thought*, edited by Marcia J. Bunge..., 450-455.

[56] The rights contained in the United Conventions on Convention for Rights of Children (UNCRC) can be classified into four broad categories. They are Subsistence rights, Development rights, Protection rights and Participation rights. While the UNCRC emphasises that the family is the natural environment for nurturing the child, it places the primary obligation on the state to protect children from all forms of abuse, neglect and exploitation, even where these are not carried out directly by state agents. In this way, the CRC challenges the traditional

involved in decision-making and participation in required situations).[57]

India is one of the countries that signed the United Nations Convention on Child's Rights with reservation regarding child labour in 1992. However, during the last few years, there has been a progressive attitude towards children's rights. The problem of child labour has been getting serious attention after a historic judgment by the Supreme Court of India in 1996, which prescribed a fine of Rs. 20,000 for employing child labour in prohibited areas. This judgment is of serious concern as hardly any prosecution took place under this category until 1998. Nothing eye-opening has happened since then.

The law of the land has prescribed freedom to knowledge about existing laws for one's existence and the freedom to express

---

perception that states are not responsible for abuses committed within the family or the community. Domestic violence, bonded child labour or child prostitution, for instance, are usually perpetrated by private individuals, but governments can be held accountable for failing in their responsibilities to protect children from such abuses because government has the right to intervene. Subsistence rights contains the rights to food, shelter and health care; development rights allow children to reach their fullest potential, including education and freedom of thought, conscience and religion; Protection rights, such as the right to life, and to protection from abuse, neglect or exploitation; and Participation rights allow children to take an active role in community and political life. 1989 UN Declaration on the Rights of the Child, *http://www.unhchr.ch/html/menu3/b/25.htm* (25 Oct. 2007).

[57] Quoted from Hammarberg T by Rudi Roose and Maria Bouverne-de Bie, "Do Children have Rights or Do their Rights have to be Realised? The United Nation Convention on the Rights of the Child as a Frame of Reference for Pedagogical Action", *Journal of Philosophy of Education* 41/3 (2007): 431. Also, see Annemie Dillen, "Children between Liberation and Care: Ethical Perspectives on the Right of Children and Parent-Child Relationships", *International Journal of Children Spirituality* 11/2 (Aug. 2006): 237-250.

one's state of being (especially the circumstances of exploitation) and the consequences for the violation of the same. Here, the practice of untouchability in any form is an offense punishable in accordance with law. Two important legislations were made by the Parliament in relation to this article: (i) The Untouchablity (Offense) Act, 1955—renamed as Protection of Civil Rights act, 1955, in 1976, and (ii) the Schedule Castes and Schedule Tribes (Prevention of Atrocities) Act, 1989. Article 23 prohibits trafficking of human beings, which includes forcing children to labour. Article 45 of the Indian Constitution directs education as a right for children and not a privilege. However, discriminatory forces deprive the very education that empowers one to express one's situation. The ever-alarming rate of enrolment of children in schools and equally alarming rate of dropouts remain. Worse so for girl-children, as the dropout rate as compared to male children is dreadful.[58]

The constitution expressly prohibits employment of children below fourteen years especially in factories or mines or any other hazardous work. The right to life (including the right to livelihood) and the right to live in dignity and security are deemed as paramount among rights. Denial of survival and development, freedom of expression causing harm of neglect and exploitation of children in any form, is a violation of the right to live with dignity and the right of protection against exploitation. Employment of children thus violates the essence of Article 21. A further directive in this regard is that children shall be provided education up to 14 years; it is now their fundamental right to be in school. Free and compulsory education is a fundamental right

---

[58] Indian Social Institute, *State of Human Rights in India 1998* (New Delhi: ISI, 1999).

for all children between 6 and 14 years. An extension of this argument can be that the denial of primary education would lead children to work, which is a hazard by itself.[59]

Non-discrimination among children is one of the most guaranteed gestures provided by Article 14. It combines with Article 24 (prohibiting employment) and Article 15 (State empowered to make any special law for children). It also guarantees that the child must be given the opportunity and facility to develop in a healthy manner, that the tender age of the child is not abused and that citizens are not forced by economic necessity to enter avocations unsuited to their age or strength.

Role of Monitoring Agencies

The dual objectives that are aimed at by the monitoring agencies are:

- The State smoothens promotion and realisation of human rights and rights of children.

- Protecting the promoters (individuals and agencies) from excesses and abuses of the State.

On the contrary, lethargy of conviction and systemic institutionalisation seem to have crept in. For instance, in 2004, the Committee on Rights of Children indicated a preference for progressive elimination of child labour. However, this was a "top-heavy" model of implementing, which was internationally well-

---

[59] The Right to Education Bill, 2009, sets 6-14 as the eligible age-group for education, subtly shrugging off children on either ends of the cut-off ages. Those falling between 1-6 and later 14-atleast 18 are assumed either too early for "education" or too late to imbibe any knowledge and wisdom for their future. Such discourses have restricted the definition of "education" as well as "childhood" just to the activities within the four walls of the school (assuming that all schools in India have a minimum of four walls and a safe roof!).

structured but found wanting at grass roots locations. At the national level, it has been observed that these committees follow a bureaucratic model of non-confrontation even on matters of serious violations and abuses. At best, they persuade the government to take note of the issue and offer suggestions for follow-up action. These monitoring activities seem to be accountable more to international bodies than to domestic constituencies.[60]

Sharda observes at least three limitations of law-framing, law-enforcing and law-monitoring agencies:

1. Lawmakers are to a great deal unaware of the ground reality while framing laws.

2. The laws so far framed are applicable largely to the organised sector, whereas the unorganised sectors escape scrutiny.

3. The enforcement machinery is seen in participatory collusion with the exploiters of child labour.[61]

So, current child labour policies fail to address the exclusion of children from the production of value and reinforce paradoxically children's vulnerability to exploitation.

Independent India has approached the cause of labouring children in stages. V. R. Krishna Iyer discerns this callousness and reveals how India has come under the severe scanner of the United Nations for its largely disinterested ways to give effect to the U. N. Convention on the Rights of the child and yet calling itself a

---

[60] Archana Mehendale, 'Children's Rights: Lessons on Monitoring," *Economic and Political Weekly* Vol XXXIX No. 16 (April 17-23, 2004): 1568-1570

[61] Neel K. Sharda, *The Legal, Economic and Social Status...*, 23. For the similar ideas expressed, See, *The Hindu*, Kochi (10 Aug. 2007), 14.

Socialist Republic. He blames Union Governments for promoting "silent terrorism [and] tactic debunking of humanism" and for its "societal criminality and culpable desertification of fertile human resources."[62]

Operational Positions of Discourses on the Rights and their Gendered Construction

Let us take a look at the operational positions of discourses on rights and their gendered construction.

1. The concept of International Labour Laws and Standards tend to universalise the parameters of definitions of "child labour." In the process, the life situation of the labouring children of the West is treated as definitional for theorising crucial policies. Here all countries are expected to stick to these policies. Conversely, with the emergence of the phenomenon of child labour under inevitable circumstances, the compelling debate on its elimination is uncalled for.[63] The conceptualisation of work and its cultural meaning are significant in evaluating and accepting the definition of child labour. Olga Niewenhuys feels that the two-thirds world depends largely on the western legislation on child labour, which makes distinction between "harmful and suitable (if

---

[62] V. R. Krishna Iyer, "Needed, a Code of Child Rights," *The Hindu* (Kochi), 14 November 2007, 11.

[63] Niewenhuys suggests at least two ulterior motives in the earlier call for the elimination of child labour: (1) There was a desire to protect the initiatives to mechanise the textile industry from the uncontrolled competition of the labour force comprised almost entirely of children; (2) there was also a fear of political instability created by a youthful working class not to be disciplined by the army, schools or the church. Olga Niewenhuys, "The Paradox of Child Labour and Anthropology," OICSSA, edited by Veena Das (New Delhi: Oxford University Press, 2003), 940- 941.

not desirable) work."[64] At the rehabilitation front, while children and their families submissively and vulnerably wait upon the State's intervention, the due privilege does not seep down to the real sufferers.

2. The assessment of enforcement and monitoring agencies is imperative. Deepti Sukumar points out the deliberate attempts to defocus the loss of link between liberation and rehabilitation.[65] One of the often-discussed issues with regard to laws on child labour—or their violation—is the vigilant responsibility of regulatory bodies in dealing with these matters. Also, what needs equally important attention, as laws on child labour, are the laws that address issues of caste-based and other determinant-based dehumanising discrimination. The emancipation of children from inhuman situation can stem from the constant ulterior constructive interaction between the legal machinery and cultural ethos. Intriguingly, here one can notice the constant struggle between two powerful allies to pull each other to their sides. One that controls caste-based activities is strongly embedded in culture for centuries and, therefore, being treated as normative. The other, the jurisprudence, formulated largely on the value-based ideals that would ensure equal footing for all citizens regardless of any personal allegiance to any caste-centred drills.

3. That human rights is a Western construct, one can only say with great certainty that an uncritical treatment of human rights for the issues of child labour would only involve colonial

---

[64] Niewenhuys, "The Paradox of Child Labour and Anthropology,"…, 941.

[65] Deepthi Sukumar, "The Safaikarmacharis in the Body of Christ," in *Frontiers in Dalit Hermeneutics*, edited by James Massey and Samson Prabhakar (Bangalore/Delhi: BTESSC-SATHRI/CDSS, 2005), 25

project and encounter. As Geeta Chowdhry explains, "The 1948 Universal Declaration of Human Rights... is seen by critics as rooted in the experience of the Enlightenment, the particularities of a post Second World War Europe, and the dominance of the United States in the international political economy."[66] Therefore, they "have become symbolic and expedient tools of identity marking, as well as tools of inclusion and exclusion in discourses of resistance."[67] It can be noticed with regret that the place of child in human rights, as in any other discourse, is "rooted in the exclusions."

4.   A prudent survey of the real-life condition of child labourers in India would lead us to the fact that, unfortunately, culturally accepted norms like caste, class and gendered notions have prevailed over the constitutionally accepted ways only because the powerful have made their way into policy-making bodies and those in power have been the beneficiaries of such politics. And they, in return, feel obliged to legitimise and sustain such norms. Or, as Dirks observes, the ideology of caste and other determinants consists of and is institutionalised in a collection of bodies like religious groups, education or schooling, and civic establishments that simultaneously embody the interests of those in power and are cushioned by State-run machineries. Especially, caste as a product of religious principles has tentacled political organisations.[68] The underlying discourse in all these debates is fundamentally one of locating the organising theme of centrality of power and the powerful. Power, here, either

---

[66] Geeta Chowdhry, "Postcolonial Interrogations," ..., 231.

[67] Geeta Chowdhry, "Postcolonial Interrogations," ..., 231.

[68] Nicolas B Dirks, "The Invention of Caste: Civil Society in Colonial India," in *Identity, Consciousness and the Past: Forging of Caste and Community in India and Sri Lanka,* edited by Seneviratne H.L. (Delhi: Oxford University Press, 1999), 124

manifests without any coercion from any one front or ingeniously uses policy makers to put up its front.

5.   The question of autonomy of children is a crucial question to handle, just as crucial as the question of their protection. We continue to find out which is a child domain and which an adult one. Again, where and on what issues can we draw lines between adult rights and child rights? What if children have complete rights but no forums to claim their provisions? How much can they represent themselves until the "ideal" egalitarian world materialises? Until then do they not need adult assistance/facilitations through rights—forums?

Analysing Power Dynamics in Child Labour Debates

The life-world of children both within and outside immediate social units of children has been thoroughly colonised by the values of the marketplace, values that happen to be chiefly agential and adult.[69] Here what one can re-vision is that:

> Every child labourer is a child with all the needs of other children. He [*sic*] needs opportunity for growth not [only] for physical, but [also] in mind and personality, through all the activities, and experiences, which properly belong to childhood, when the business of wage earning, or of participation in self or family support, conflicts directly or indirectly with the business of growth and education, the social evil of children evident. [70]

Recent anthropological approaches and application of new critical tools like postmodern and postcolonial approaches detect the murkiness of "global" visions of childhood that deliberately or otherwise connive in grass-roots debates and constantly prohibit children in the production of value and identity. This question

---

[69] As quoted by John Wall in John Wall, "Childhood Studies, Hermeneutics, and Theological Ethics," *JR* 86/ 4 (Oct. 2006), 544.

[70] *ECFW*, vol. 4:..., 16.

does not favor child labour but deliberates on how we could reorganise the concerns of labouring children and their childhood in India. Olga Niewenhuys, an anthropologist, highlights the paradox inherent in such child labour talks. While the global discourse represents childhood through the ideals of innocence, she argues that one could recast the discourses on child labour in terms of its inability to address the question of exclusion of children from remunerative employment.[71]

Of discursive importance here is the "identity" discourse created in the context of deprived opportunities of child labourers. These identities could be redefined for the benefit of these children if the children are offered due privileges and opportunities as other privileged children. Amartya Sen values the freedom of each individual "not merely because it assists achievement, but also because of its own importance, going beyond the value of the state of existence actually achieved."[72] In other words, the loss of opportunity is the loss of freedom, which, in turn, is the loss of some importance that directly hampers children's ability to lay claim on their much-desired childhood benefits. Therefore, the concentration should be on alternative social arrangements that critically evaluate a "less just" or "more just" situation than on a

---

[71] Niewenhuys argues that the governments, while condemning the relatively uncommon forms of waged labour as exploitation, sanctioned a broad spectrum of other activities like house keeping, child minding, helping adults for no pay, working in family farms and shops, delivering newspapers, seasonal works in farms and workshops. This establishes borderline between morally desirable and pedagogically sensible activities, on one hand, and the exploitation of children, on the other. Niewenhuys, "The Paradox of Child Labour and Anthropology,"..., 937.

[72] Amartya Sen, *On Ethics and Economics*, (New Delhi: Oxford University Press, 1987), 60.

transcendental ideal of a fully just society.[73] Sen makes a strong case for a revised role of the state in the educational sector. He mentions that schooling of any standard generally has had a positive impact on children but should lay "emphasis on coverage over quality education." This is how the networking of State and philanthropists could work to provide opportunities toward a common good.[74]

Geeta Chowdhry, through the lens of postcolonial hermeneutics, situates child labour "not only in the internationalization of global economy, but also in the gendered constructions of a globalized economy. [It] foregrounds race, gender, and class and their imbrication with the capital, knowledge, and representation that surrounds child labour"[75] She notices that the orthodox liberal political economy and Marxist political economy emphasise on the production and consumption of the commodities, but does not delve into the subsumed identities and "representational issue" attached to material analysis. While most approaches "ignore the racialized, gendered, and class basis of this identity,"[76] emancipatory discourses should seek "to uncover 'the operations of power in relation to knowledge formation' and codification that existed historically and 'that are emerging in the contexts of globalization at the turn of the century."[77]

---

[73] Amartya Sen, "What do we want from a Theory of Justice?" *JP* CIII/ 5, (May 2006), 216.

[74] "Stress on Education", *The Hindu* (Kochi), (20 December 2007), 1.

[75] Geeta Chowdhry, "Postcolonial Interrogations,"…, 228.

[76] Geeta Chowdhry, "Postcolonial Interrogations,"…, 228.

[77] Geeta Chowdhry, "Postcolonial Interrogations,"…, 233.

Conclusion

In the current context, the paradox of globalisation as a phenomenon has brought not only more information about the plight of child labour, but also goods produced by children in far away lands into the hands of consumers in high-income countries. Globalisation, in its working style in India, seems to have either uncritically inculturated the norms traditionally followed in deciding who the labouring classes should be or is by design in concurrence with traditional determinants like caste, class and gender. On the other hand, regardless of innovative and critical influences, one factor that has stood its ground prominently and that needs reassessment is the strong caste-undercurrent that determines from which caste or community would the child labourers come. As appraised and presented in this chapter, a majority of them still come from Scheduled Castes, Scheduled Tribes, Other Backward Castes and Muslim communities. From among these communities, it is observed that Dalit children are sought after, more often than not, to perpetuate *status quo* at various realms of societal functioning.

Uneasy over these issues, different groups of people and individuals who are genuinely concerned about the plight of child labourers in the two-thirds world and those who comprise the forces of protectionism from various parts of the world have assumed responsibilities to theoretically and practically tackle the intrigues involved. While it is plausible that child labour cannot be eliminated, alternative approaches are in place to confront the "systemic fallacy." One can readily agree with Deepthi Sukumar's view that there is, somehow, a deliberate breach of deliberations between liberation and rehabilitation in various realms.[78] If caste system in India has a strong say in the issues of child labour, how

---

[78] Deepthi Sukumar, "The Safaikarmacharis in the Body of Christ,"..., 25.

have our liberation discourses in theology failed to address these questions? Ironically, even liberation theology in India is yet to succeed in "standing in the breach" (Ezek. 22. 30). Our theologies should bridge these breaches to stake claims for their relevance.

CHAPTER 2

Children and *Labour* in Christian Thought

With the pressing need to theologically address the issue of child labour, this section attempts to retrieve and reclaim the place and role of children in the biblical and theological discourses presented to date. This evaluation reposits beyond the conventional dimensions of child as a metaphor towards the concept of childhood as a significant stage in itself. This assessment reveals how a theological slip like the insignificant attention to the issues of children and childhood has drastically affected our views on child labourers. This assessment also facilitates in formulating affirmative positions on children and, consequently, child labourers. Equally significant is the assessment of the issue of labour that would help us to devise theological discourse on child labour.

Biblical Understanding of the Child: Recovering Childhood

The Hebrew scripture offers a plethora of constructs of childhood in its socio-cultural milieu. Therefore, one notices a deep rift at, at least, two levels: Between the conception and organisation of "childhood" in different socio-cultural traditions presented in the Hebrew Scriptures and between the high, idealistic theological significance of children and the real-life situation of children of the age. The theological importance of children such as "children as a gift from God," "means of God's activity," and "a symbolic assurance of the covenant between God and the people of Israel"[1] inclined the Hebrews to have children and to place them in high esteem. The psalmist, on this front, draws attention to the fact that young children are capable of worshipping God and participating in community faith affirmations (Ps. 8: 2- 3). Socially, culturally and politically, children were, however, the powerless ones and were on the bottom rung of Hebrew and other ancient societal set-ups. Traditions and customs perpetuated privileged positions to adults and older people (Prov. 16:31; Job 12:12). The following discussions are elaborations of these conceptions.

In the Hebrew culture of biblical times, children immortalised the family heritage and the covenantal promise of God. Childlessness was shameful, and measures were taken to overcome this situation. The worth of a woman was established by her ability to bear children. The Sarah-Abraham narrative towards having Isaac presents God as helping out a woman of shame. The promise to the couple is fulfilled by the divine intervention when their aged physic had almost negated the possibilities, especially even after Abraham had already worked towards immortalising his lineage by having Ishmael through Hagar. The Levirate law promulgated that in the instances of childlessness, the law provided for carrying on the family name and for continuity through the nearest relative (Deut. 25:5-10).[2] Covenantally, God guaranteed the continuance of Abraham's

---

[1] Joseph A. Grassi, "Child, Children", *ABD* vol. 1, edited by David Noel Freedman (New York: Doubleday, 1992), 904- 907. Also see, the etymological description of Children in the Hebrew Scriptures (OT) and the New Testament under the titles '*Yonek,*' and '*Tap,*' in *NIDOTTE*, edited by William A. VanGemeren, vol 2 (Grand Rapids, Michigan: Zondervan Publishing House, 1997), and '*Helikia,*' '*Pais,*' and '*Nepios,*' in *NIDNTT,* edited by Colin Brown, vol. 1 (Grand Rapids, Michigan: Zondervan Publishing House: 1986).

[2] Joseph A. Grassi, "Child, Children,"..., 904- 907

legacy by giving him descendants (through children) as innumerable as the dust of the earth and the stars of the heavens (Gen. 12:2, 13:6, 15:5). The desire for children, and children as a gift and a great source of joy to family and community, have many anecdotes.[3] The Psalmist emphasises this 'more-the-children-the-greater-the-joy' tradition (Ps. 127:3-5, 128:3-6).

Children and the Expected Messiah

The image of the 'child' plays an important part in messianic expectations. Isaiah announces about a future *child* of David's line who will be the hope of his people despite much suffering (7:14, 16; 9:16). The same prophet also describes this future in terms of an idyllic return to the childlike innocence of the Garden of Eden (11:8–9). The prophet Zechariah has a vision of the messianic era as a time of peace and joy when "the streets of the city shall be full of boys and girls playing in them" (8:5).[4] Evidently, male children received greater attention in both the social and religious realms of the Hebrew society. Infant males received the sign of the covenant through circumcision (Gen. 17:10-14) and were expected to take up covenantal responsibilities. This bias led to the expectation of covenantal initiations largely through male children and, consequently, the expectation of only a male messiah.

Parent-Child Relationship

At the sociological level, parents had almost absolute authority over children. Children were educated through strict obedience

---

[3] In one such instance, according to a second-century rabbinic tradition, a rabbi who was observed crawling on his hands and feet with a reed in his mouth and following his son, explained his behaviour by saying, "You see that when a man [sic] loves to have children, he acts like a fool." (*Midrash* Ps. 92, 14.206b), cited by Hans-Ruedi Weber, *Jesus and the Children: Biblical Resources for Study and Preaching* (Geneva: World Council of Churches, 1979), 11-12.

[4] Joseph A.Grassi, "Child, Children,"…, 904- 907.

often enforced by severe physical punishment (Prov. 13:24; 19:18; 22:15; 23:13). The law reinforced parental authority with its own strong sanctions (Exod. 21:17; Lev. 20:9).[5] Adults thought of children as always falling short of the "ideal" standard as set by the adult, male, law-observant Israelite. Where children could not live up to the set expectations, they were constantly referred to as "deaf and dumb, weak minded and under age… [and] not in full possession of their intellectual powers."[6] Children as at complete mercy of their parents are well depicted in many narratives. Abraham was willing to sacrifice his promised son Isaac to live up to his stature as a leader of his community. Jepthah's unwaveringly stuck to his vow to sacrifice even his only child, a girl (Judg. 11). During the economic crunch of the Israelites, some members of the community had to pledge their children for debt-slavery.[7] Mesha, the Moabite king, was fighting a loosing battle with his best seven hundred swordsmen. Then he burnt his son, who was supposed to succeed him, as an offering and the result turned in his favor.

Drawing from such experiences, Hebrew scripture writers use the image of the child for "helplessness" (Num. 11:12), "hopelessness," "weakness" and "lack of significance" (Isa. 53:2; Lam. 4: 4). The child was also a symbol of vulnerability (Gen. 34: 29; Num. 31:9, 18). Theologically, children's helplessness was thought of having a logical association with their "immaturity" and "less knowledge," which in turn placed their parents and other

---

[5] Joseph A. Grassi, "Child, Children,"…, 904- 907.

[6] As found in Rabbinic Literature, cited by Judith M. Gundry-Wolf, "The Least and the Greatest: Children in the New Testament," in *The Child in Christian Thought*, edited by Marcia J. Bunge (Michigan/ Cambridge: William B. Eerdmans Publishing Company, 2001), 35.

[7] Williamson, H.G.M., *Word Biblical Commentary, Volume 16: Ezra, Nehemiah*, (Dallas, Texas: Word Books, Publisher) 1998.

adults as protectors or patrons. These roles subtly turned to "predators" as well.

The reforms during Nehemiah depict a movement to challenge an unjust and an anti- covenant motif as far as children are concerned. During the economic crunch of the Israelites, some members of the community had to pledge their children for debt-slavery.[8] They belonged to landless classes and had to mortgage whatever little property they owned. Under compulsions, they treated their children as exchange goods, similar to our own situation where debt-trapped parents drive children into the labour force, all the more in a neo-colonial context. In that situation, as it is mostly now, this psychologically built-in phenomenon of converting a child into a commodity seemed to be an "alright" adult logic! Indeed, the process was already starting, as some of their daughters had already been "enslaved" to sexually gratify the creditors' lusts as payment for delaying foreclosure on the loans. This word in Hebrew has sexual overtones (as in Esther 7:8)[9], and the singling out of daughters here suggests more severe treatment separate from debt-slavery. This kind of singling out of girls could be noticed in temple prostitution where girl-children have paid a greater price. Such glaring internal colonies challenge our theological complacency.

Are children economic entities who, with the least idea of what happens around them, compete to give in meekly to the world of adults? Naomi Steinberg, analysing the social-construct and economic motivations in the narrative of young Samuel in 1 Samuel, reiterates the economic intensions of parents as adults that ruthlessly prevailed over children's vulnerability in the

---

[8] Williamson, H.G.M., *Word Biblical Commentary, Volume 16: Ezra, Nehemiah*, (Dallas, Texas: Word Books, Publisher) 1998.

[9] Williamson, H.G.M., *Word Biblical Commentary, Volume 16: Ezra, Nehemiah*, (Dallas, Texas: Word Books, Publisher) 1998.

Hebrew scriptures. Hannah's prayer for the gift of a child, while appearing to be religiously motivated, is also economically motivated. This adult motivation is legitimised as God's own interest, who, it appears, needs a replacement for Eli's sons. Thus, according to this analysis, the "property paradigm" of childhood is well explicated in this instance: infant Samuel is merely a pawn in Hanna's move to "be bartered away to Yahweh in exchange for the gift of fertility, followed by her expected subsequent rise in status in the family of her husband Elkanah."[10] Steinberg says:

> In an economic sense, a child's value and identity was formed based on membership in a family, i.e., a patrilineage, and what the child owes the parent based on this family identity. The economic value of a child is seen, e.g., in 2 Kgs 4:1, when children are taken by a creditor to pay off a debt. Control over a child's fate resides in the hands of the child's parents when the child is viewed as property. By the same token, in the case of Samuel, his dedication to Yahweh at Shiloh requires making a sacrifice as his parents fulfill Hannah's vow. Individual actions, in a context such as this one, where family values address economic production and reproduction, represent collective family interests.[11]

The Child in Greco-Roman Culture and Society

The primary identity of children depended on the family into which they were born. The children's specific position was defined through the socio-economic system and the role of family in the system. Children who were born into the household of slaves became slaves by birth and the property of the masters of the

---

[10] Naomi Steinberg's "1 Samuel 1, the United Nations Convention on the Rights of Children, and 'The Best Interests of the Child' *Journal of Childhood and Religion* Volume 1, Issue 3 (April 2010): 12 (1- 23) is one of the lastest works on the Rights of Children and its reading of the Hebrew Scriptures.

[11] Naomi Steinberg, "1 Samuel 1, the United Nations Convention"…
13

household. Children usually became the property of the mothers'
masters. They were allowed to accumulate and manage separate
property. But they could not own any property because whatever
they acquired belonged to their master.[12] Children carried on the
family name and business and provided care for elderly parents.
Intellectually, children were treated as lacking in reason and,
therefore, adults-in-the-making that required training, which
included physical battering.[13] While children were also valued as
individuals and enjoyed parental love and affection, the
households followed the patriarchal norms that greatly benefited
male children. Usually the father, the supreme head of the family
and its business, had the final say in familial matters, especially
in deciding either to keep or "expose" the child, especially a girl-
child. It was a Roman custom to place a newborn on the ground
in front of the father for him to inspect whether he could accept
or reject the child. Such infanticide practices as exposing children
were never sanctioned and never condemned by the Roman law.
Exposure had a long history and was advocated by philosophers
too.[14] It was a harsh practice that was widespread during this

---

[12] David C. Verner, *The Household of God: The Social World of the
Pastoral Epistles* (California: Scholars Press, 1983), 34.

[13] Plato states: "Of all the wild beasts, the child is the most intractable;
for insofar as it, above all others, possesses a fount of reason that is as
yet uncurbed, it is a treacherous, sly and most insolent creature.
Wherefore the child must be strapped up, as it were, with many bridles"
(Plato *Leg.*, 808D), cited by D. L. Stamps, "Children in Late Antiquity,"
DNTB, edited by Craig A. Evans and Stanley E. Porter (Downers Grove,
IL: Inter-Varsity Press, 2000), 197.

[14] Plato *Rep.* 460 C; Plutarch *Lyc.* 16.1; cf. Philo *Spec. Leg.* 3.110 –119),
in D. L. Stamps, "Children in Late Antiquity,"..., 198. Also see, Hans-
Ruedi Weber, *Jesus and the Children...*, 6-7. Weber also mentions that
'Exposure' was abhorable to Jewish traditions as they treated children
as blessings from God (Ps. 127: 3-5). See Hans Ruedi- Weber, "The
Gospel in the Child," *ER* 31/ 3, (1979): 229.

period, specially the "exposure" of "unwanted" children—
particularly girls—in public places. Those who "survived" such
exposure were raised into a vicious circle of slavery, beggary and
prostitution," and many girl-children were raised for "special"
roles as temple prostitutes in cultic settings for their less rational
nature and sexual purity.[15] Moreover, many of the cheap labourers
were either themselves the prisoners of war or the children of such
prisoners. Many were bought in the slave market. Of them some
girls were given the role of a mother to breed more children for
slavery.[16] This fuelled the vicious circle of girl-children exploitation
as disposable creatures among Greeks and Romans.[17]

---

[15] J. L. White, *Light from Ancient Letters*, cited by Gundry-Volf, *Children as Recipients of the Reign of God...*, 33. See also, Everett Ferguson, *Backgrounds of Early Christianity*, 2nd ed. (Grand Rapids, Michigan: William B. Eerdmans Publishing Company, 1993), 73-74; See Hans Ruedi- Weber, "The Gospel in the Child"..., 228.

[16] Everett Ferguson, *Backgrounds of Early Christianity...*, 56.

[17] John Eastburn Boswell in his article *"Expositio* and *Oblatio:* The Abandonment of Children and the Ancient and Medieval Family" argues that exposing a child to risk was not the intention of the parents but to "offer the child up- to the kindness of strangers, to the mercy of the gods, to public welfare, to a better fate (than the natal parent could offer), or simply to his [child's] chances... *Expositio* was an *alternative* to infanticide." While Boswell agrees that such exposed children were picked up for slavery and pushed into such harsher lives, he argues his case from a non- infanticide perspective. Therefore, for Boswell it is morally better for parents to expose their children that to strangulate them. He cites instances where a child is abandoned in a basket on the water or a child born out of rape or incest is left aside on a road side. Here, one can again notice the either/or options argued out from the perspective of the adults (parents) with least attention to the children at risk. This forms of arguments also bring to light the researches take up for centuries purely from adults eyes while sidelining the right of livelihood of children.

With regard to the education of children, those of wealthy parents could afford formal education that included learning to write, read and handle basic arithmetic, often combined with physical education. Beating was a common practice to infuse discipline. Among those who crossed the age of twelve, only boys could continue their education while girls were trained in the "expected duties" of a female in a household. Home was the first school for training in religious traditions and ritual.

Children in the Teachings of Jesus

In the many texts on "children"[18] in the New Testament, rarely are children discussed apart from adults. Judith Gundry-Volf[19] and Hans-Reudi Weber have explored the centrality of the theme of children in Jesus' teachings where the children-Jesus interaction could pose "radical challenges to adult Christians" to evolve significant models for Christian theology and mission to understand children better.

The Child and the Reign of God

In Jesus' teachings, the association of children is emphatically with the Reign of God. This section takes up the stance of the reign of God-children relationship to accentuate the significance of children's lives by evaluating the concerned gospel passages. Gundry-Volf culls out the following significance of children: Children are the inheritors of the reign of God; they are models of entering the reign of God; they are the paradigms of greatness in the reign of God; receiving children is as significant as receiving Jesus; and exemplary humility of children is required of any

---

[18] As Weber suggests, such expressions "refer to a relationship or specify the origin of a person" rather than the age. See, Hans Reudi-Weber, *Jesus and the Children*, especially the exegetical details in the appendices, 52- 94.

[19] Gundry-Volf, "The Least and the Greatest,"..., 29- 58.

person in God's reign. Weber's aim, on the other hand, is to pull out lessons from Jesus' outlook of children for wider significance especially for "adult Christian life."

Jesus' blessing of children and pronouncement of their place in the reign of God attract great attention, especially in a period where desertion of children was not a misdemeanor. Jesus categorically invites little children to come to him and to be "among" them (Matt. 19: 13-15, Mark 10: 13-16 and Luke 18: 15-17). He vehemently reverses the disciples' intentions to keep children on the margins! (Mark 10:14). His indignation suggests the gravity of the exclusion of children from God's blessings. Even as he takes them up in his arms and blesses them (Mark 10:16), he performs the practice of the laying on of hands, which is one to announce that children are dedicated to be a part of God's reign and that they too are members of the community of faith. More remarkably, little children can serve as a paradigm for the conduct of disciples. Furthermore, Jesus' words, "Let them come to me" resonates the core of Christian community living.

Jesus uses novel ways to teach his disciples about entering the kingdom of God. An invitation to Jesus—and the one who sent him—could be through welcoming a child to be "among them" (Luke 9:46). The thought "Kingdom of God" as "Kingdom of children" has attracted various perceptions. It was this defenselessness and helplessness that prompted Crossan to state sarcastically that this "kingdom of children" is the "kingdom of nobodies" for "to be a child was nobody."[20]

---

[20] John Dominic Crossan, *The Historical Jesus: The Life of a Mediterranean Jewish Peasant* (San Francisco: Harper, 1991), 265- 302.

Sacramentality of the Child: The Child in Early Church

In the early church, firstly, the cultural patriarchy and the social structure of the household dictated the significance of children. Secondly, they were accepted as lesser beings of the Christian community, representing the immature Christian spirituality. Therefore, childhood was a category of lesser theological and social significance.

A common perception of the epistles is that a child symbolises a stage that one is to grow out of (i.e., the present stage as a stage of immaturity) or a state of being where one's potential is not completely realised (1 Cor. 13:11; 14:20; Heb. 5:13; 1 Peter 2:2). Here, the difference between Jesus' teaching and the teachings in the epistles about children is an interesting point of theological and historical musing. Paul's use of the theological metaphor of children as someone to mature towards adulthood (1 Cor. 4:14-15; Gal. 4:19; 1 Thess. 2:11) and the impression of the writer of the Johannine epistles about children (1 John 2:1, 18, 28; 3:7, 18; 5:21) represent the authors' spiritual association with social reality, both implicitly and explicitly. They deprive children of their sacramental presence as full members of the Body of Christ and as Images of God.

At the social level, children were generally positioned within the household codes of the day (Eph. 6:1-4; Col. 3:20-21; 1 Tim. 5:4) where parents reinforced the notion of disciplining and instructing them (1 Tim. 3:4, 12; Titus 1:6). This household imagery was perhaps extended to the concept of the Body of Christ, where the fullness of Christ was comprehended in the image of grown up persons (Eph. 4:13), in contrast to the child, who could be easily handled and influenced (Eph. 4:14).[21] The imagery of children ('pais') (Matt. 8:6, 13; Luke 7:7; 12:43; 12: 45; 1 Cor. 14:20; I Peter 2:2) was also used to depict the least-solicited position of slaves in the society.

---

[21] R. Schippers, "Helikia," *NIDNTT,* edited by Colin Brown, vol. 1…, 92- 93.

On the other hand, the positive regard for children as in the Jewish perspective is also evident when Paul indicates that children of Christian parents are "holy" (1 Cor. 7:14) and that fathers should not provoke their children (Eph.6:1-4). Participation of and instructions to children in the Acts (2:39), epistles to Ephesians and Colossians presuppose their participation in Christian assemblies.

Evangelist Mathew derogatorily introduces the 'insignificant' presence of children in religious gatherings such as in the feeding of the 'five thousand men' (14:21, cf. Matt. 15:38), although the source of nourishment and sustenance through that meal pointed directly to the 'sacramental' sharing of the food by a young boy. In this incident, scholars have associated sacramental significance to the prayer and act of Jesus of distributing the food.[22] They substantiate it by pointing out that "Jesus is the messianic provider" and that the "messianic blessing also appears to be intended in the overabundance of food."[23] Grossly forgotten is the boy as the "provider" and that the abundance of the food had its beginning in the sharing of the boy's food! Unfortunately, scholars could not see a messianic act of sharing of the subsistence in the act of this child.

Epistemological Dynamics to Reclaim the Place of Children

Matt. 18:2-5 provides a model of humility as exhibited by children and how such emulation leads one to receive the knowledge of

---

[22] New Testament Scholars such as C. H. Dodd and X. Leon- Dufour take this position. George R. Beasely- Murray, "John," *WBC* vol 36, edited by David A. Hubbard and Glenn W. Barker (Dallas, Texas: Word Books Publisher, 1998).

[23] Donald A. Hagner, "Matthew", *WBC* vol 33b, edited by David A. Hubbard and Glenn W. Barker (Dallas, Texas: Word Books Publisher, 1998), 418- 419.

God.[24] However, the one that challenges the paradigm that hitherto equates 'wisdom' with 'adults' is Luke 10: 21 (par. Matt. 11:25), which presents the prayer of Jesus:

> I thank you, Father, Lord of heaven and earth, because you have hidden these things from the wise and the intelligent and have revealed them to infants; yes, Father, such was your gracious will.

While it is argued that the use of the word "children" (in Latin meaning "the one who cannot speak", or "voiceless"[25]) here—as elsewhere in many of the elucidated passages—can have only metaphorical significance, a latent significance is a new epistemological movement. Conventionally, a common purpose of "raising" children was to make them reach adulthood as adulthood epitomised maturity, rationality and power. Therefore, childhood was only a means of reaching adulthood and not a valuable stage of life in itself. The child's process of acquiring knowledge was to move towards the knowledge that adults could comprehend and possess. However, the above-cited passage strikes the bottom of that prerogative. The passage implies a new methodology where the epistemological movement is from child to adult and not only vice versa, as conventionally believed. Here,

---

[24] To become a child, in the Gospel of Thomas, is to "become a single one". Here, when the presumed dichotomies like the inner- outer, male-female, or above- below are overcome in a person, then that person can enter the kingdom of God. Howard C. Kee, "'Becoming a Child' in the Gospel of Thomas," *JBL* 82/ 3 (Sep. 1963): 307-314. Stable URL:

http://links.jstor.org/sici?sici=00219231per cent28196309per cent2982per cent3A3per cent3C307per cent3Aper cent22ACITGper cent3E2.0.COper cent3B2-0 (Tue Jan 22 01:00:44 2008).

[25] François Bovon, "The Child and the Beast: Fighting Violence in Ancient Christianity," *HTR* 92 / 4. (Oct. 1999): 382. Stable URL:

http://links.jstor.org/sici?sici=00178160per cent28199910per cent2992per cent3A4per cent3C369per cent3ATCATBFper cent3E2.0.COper cent3B2-P (Tue Jan 22 00:31:49 2008).

adults (implying, "the wise") are not the only custodians of knowledge or wisdom. Therefore, there is a bilateral and intergenerational interaction required of this methodology. This new methodology presents children as subjects, who would provide ways and means of attaining wisdom. So, the tag of "ignorance" from children is detached and children are made equally important in the construction of the knowledge system and in meaning-making. Children are posited with certain knowledge that has to be explored through methods that would not denigrate their existence and distinctiveness.

The new methodological thought calls for a new accompanying method, as the previous methods would comply with the previous methodologies.[26] Where *pedagogy* etymologically meant to "lead a child" (obviously by an adult towards adulthood or "towards becoming knowledgeable beings"), this scriptural passage requires one, particularly the 'wise' (the adults), to "lead oneself to a child." Enriching this methodological insight is the passage from Matt. 11: 16-19 (*cf* Luke 7: 31-35). It is an instance where Jesus discerns from a group of children playing by the street side metaphors of life and significance of such metaphors to interpret the reign of God. Jesus' willingness to learn some of his ministerial lessons through children's play is significant for having children as the centre of theological conversation.

To summarise, in a mixed bag of traditions about children that one is presented with, regrettably, only a few traditions— especially the Epistle's teachings, and more prominently, Pauline teachings on the subordination of children (as in the Protestant traditions)—have seen the light of day. It is perhaps imperative to highlight the gospel message of the centrality of children in the

---

[26] For similar discussion, see Hans Ruedi- Weber, "The Gospel in the Child,"..., 230. This research moves further from pedagogy to a wider philosophical approach by addressing the issues of epistemology.

reign of God and children as means of covenantal relationship that would help us to address the plight and demeaning position of children in our context; more so in the context where the predicament of child labourers can be addressed. It is perhaps such vulnerable children that the reign of God would rescue.

Children in Christian Theology

Generally, theological discourses have projected a "paradigmatic problem," i.e., discourses have been by adults from the perspective of adults and sustained through legitimised theologies that are "wordy, propositional and argumentative," [27] a trait supposed to be of intellectually and physically matured and "abled" persons. In the questionable hierarchy of systematic theology, children are not considered as part of the 'superior' systematic theology but of Practical Theology. Even here, the earlier discourses on children are written through parents' or community's perspectives highlighting the age bias and the peripherality of children. Discourses on children are considered to be "too dangerous and too safe, too difficult and too silly...good only for second rate minds and perhaps for women."[28]

In the second and third centuries, church teachers like Clement of Alexandria, Origen, Tertullian, Cyprian of Carthage and Gregory of Nyssa have encouraged adults to imitate children's moral simplicity, freedom from desire, sexual purity and indifference towards worldly status and wealth, but have restricted the understanding of children to these issues.[29] With modernity's

---

[27] Israel Selvanayagam, "Children Laugh and Cry: Authentic Resources for Christian Theology," *AJT* 9/2 (1995): 352

[28] Anne Higonnet, *Pictures of Innocence: The History and Crisis of Ideal Childhood* (New York: Thames & Hudson, 1998), 13- 14, cited by Bonnie J. Miller- McLemore, "Children and Religion in the Public Square: Too Dangerous and Too Safe, Too Difficult and Too Silly," *JR* 86/ 3 (July 2006): 385.

[29] John Wall, "Human Rights in Light of Children: A Christian Childist Perspective," *JPT* 17/1 (2007): 56.

dependence on science and technology, both religion and children became a private matter, therefore devaluing of their care as an essentially cultural and religious activity.[30] Even the required responsibility of parents towards children on scriptural basis was trivialised. Perhaps, such logic has led to hermeneutical dropping of the childhood lens. However, theologians like Friedrich Schleiermacher and Karl Rahner have identified children as fully human from birth and recall Jesus' respect for the full humanity of children.

Marcia Bunge discovers a "poisonous pedagogy" at the roots of such unfortunate religious teachings, just as Donald Capps observes the relation between religion and child mistreatment as "perfect together." This, as he observes in some theological writings, is because of the psychodynamic connection between physical abuse and apocalypticism.[31] In such poisonous pedagogies, the stress in on:

> ...the absolute obedience of children to parents, the sinful nature or depravity of children, and the need to 'break their wills' at a very early age with harsh physical punishment...The idea is that children are sinful and thus must have their wills 'broken' is often supported by the notions that since God demands absolute obedience to parents, even if they are acting unjustly.[32]

---

[30] Bonnie J. Miller- McLemore, "Children and Religion in the Public Square,"..., 391.

[31] Donald Capps, "Religion and Child Abuse: Perfect Together," *JSSR* 31/1(March 1992): 1- 14.

http://links.jstor.ord/sici?sici=00218294per cent28199203per cent2931per cent3A1per cent3C1per cent3ARACAPTper cent3E2.O.COper cent3B2-P (22. 1. 2008).

[32] Marcia J. Bunge, "Introduction," in *The Child in Christian Thought*, edited by Marcia J. Bunge ... 5. Also see her, "The Child, Religion and the Academy: Developing Robust Theological and Religious Understanding of Children and Childhood," *JR* 86/4 (October 2006): 549- 579.

The ensuing review evaluates the place of children in the following Christian theological themes: Children as the inheritors of the original sin and condemnation and unworthiness of children as "original sinners" without baptism. However, Jesus' dictum "Unless you become like children..." reinstates the vital significance of children.

Original Sin and Damnation

Traditionally, theology has described children as those with low human aptitude to comprehend God and to interact within the religious community. As Bunge notices, in the early Christian discourses, this "low" aptitude could be "rectified" through physical "disciplining." However, there are also cases where such condemnation is not always advocated.[33] The theology of "Original Sin" denotes the human history of guilt and gracelessness as consequent to the sin of the first humans.

The neo-Platonic views of Augustine of Hippo[34] and of John Calvin have, to a great extent, justified the infection of the original sin to children and the unforgivable conduct of adults; yet they speak about the nature of children in distinctive ways and do not recommend physically punishing children. Calvin mentions that the "whole nature" of infants is a "seed of sin" and "thus it cannot be hateful and abominable to God." However, he does not base it for his further arguments. He resorts to biblical views that infants are gifts of God and can proclaim God's goodness. However, Calvin's "seed of sin" argument had greater supporters and became operational through later Calvinists and other Protestants.[35] Jonathan

---

[33] Marcia J. Bunge, "Introduction,"... 10-11.

[34] Augustine's thoughts are highlighted and discussed in the following section on Baptism.

[35] Barbara Pitkin, "'The Heritage or the Lord': Children in the Theology of John Calvin," in *The Child in Christian Thought*, edited by Marcia J. Bunge ..., 167.

Edwards, an eighteenth-century American neo-Calvinist, exaggerates Calvin's thoughts from a Puritanist view on infant damnation and childhood depravity.[36] This led to the notion that only physical punishment was potentially destructive. To a large extent, what have gone unnoticed and uncared for are the traumatised psyche and stunted wholistic personality of mistreated children.

"Unless you become like children..."

In the context of the above-discussed theological and ecclesiastical positions on children, it is noteworthy that one of the earliest teachers, Cyprian of Carthage, and more recent theologians like Friedrich Schleiermacher and Karl Rahner could bring about a positive outlook to the place and role of children in Christian understanding "as human beings worthy of respect and dignity and as models for adults."[37] Cyprian, a third-century teacher, pictures infants as complete human beings. He asserts that across generations, all are "alike and equal since they have been made once by God." All share a "divine and spiritual equality and are able to receive God's grace and gift."[38] For Schleiermacher, children enjoy a spiritual outlook that is essential for Christian living. In their absolute helplessness and dependence, children reflect the bond between God and humanity. Trust and acceptance of dependence are natural in children, while most adults reluctantly

---

[36] Edwards explains that although infants exhibit innocence, "if they are out of Christ, they are not so in God's sight, but are young vipers, and are infinitely more hateful than vipers": as quoted by Marcia Bunge in "The Child, Religion and the Academy,"..., 564

[37] Marcia J. Bunge, "Introduction"..., 18.

[38] Cyprian of Carthage [Letter 64.3: in *Letters*, trans, Sister Rose Bernard Donna (Washington, DC: Catholic University of America Press, 1964), 217- 218], as cited by Marcia Bunge, "The Child, Religion and the Academy,"..., 566.

learn to accept their utter trust in God.[39] Karl Rahner calls childhood the beginning of openness to God or to "infinite openness." A genuine Christian experience of childhood is both realistic and idealistic. Childhood is not the first state of our biological lives, rather a basic condition appropriate to human existence lived rightly and "active as an effective force at the very roots of our being."[40]

Jurgen Moltmann, in a recent write-up has acknowledged children as "metaphors of hope."[41] He provides three hermeneutical keys to understanding children: (1) as concerned parents and teachers, (2) as children themselves and (3) as adults recalling childhood. Moltmann, however, reduces children to metaphors, signifying something outside themselves than the personalities and life of children. The individuality of children and their pressing needs and complexities of life are ignored.

Baptismal Theology and Children

An acknowledged reference to the Eastern Orthodox Baptismal Theology would be in place for an appraisal of our baptismal practices. The Syrian Church—both early and present—exhibits a largely inclusive and constructive approach with regard to the place of children in theological thought and worshipping community.[42] The earlier debates on the age of the recipients of

---

[39] Dawn DeVries, *"'Be Converted and Become as Little Children': Friedrich Schleiermacher on the Religious Significance of Childhood,"* in *The Child in Christian Thought*, edited by Marcia J. Bunge ..., 348.

[40] Mary Ann Hinsdale, *"'Infinite Openness to the Infinite': Karl Rahner's Contribution to Modern Catholic Thought on Child,"* in *The Child in Christian Thought*, edited by Marcia J. Bunge ..., 421- 445.

[41] Jurgen Moltmann, "Child and Childhood as Metaphors of Hope," *ThT* 56 (Jan. 2000): 601.

[42] The WCC's subunit- Faith and Order- has looked into the issue of admitting children to the Eucharist. Theologically, this means that even children can "have and... keep the grace of God" and "to be united with other christians". This has come up due to the "uneasiness with

baptism have given rise to divisive stances. Thomas Finn highlights how Hippolytus in his *Apostolic Tradition* makes special mention of the baptism of children ahead of everyone else, while Tertullian, a North African father, rejects infant baptism. Interestingly, Cyprian of Carthage, an ardent disciple of Tertullian, urges his congregations not even to wait the customary eight days after birth to baptise their children. However, infant and child baptisms were not ruled out. The earliest and strongest theological affirmations for infant baptism come from Origen.[43]

During the sacrament of baptism, the child is given the first Eucharist along with the Eucharistic congregation. One is baptised into the body of Christ of which the Eucharistic assembly is a manifestation. Or, in sociological terms, they are already socialised into a religious community as full members.[44] Irrespective of their age, the baptised is given the Holy Communion, which denotes the privilege of the membership in the body of Christ. Therefore,

---

the exclusion of children from a central part of the Church's life" and on a "deepened understanding of the community which christians share in Christ". Geiko Muller- Fahrenholz ed., *...And do not hinder them: An Ecumenical Plea for the admission of Children to the Eucharist* (Geneva: World Council of Churches, 1982), 4-9. However, this has not been practically implemented in most of the WCC's member churches, thus treating childhood as an inadequate period of life to receive and comprehend God's grace and to be a part of the religious community.

[43] Incorporating the baptismal liturgy as an integral part of the Eucharist liturgy symbolically signifies this position. Baptismal discourse in the early christian tradition clearly had adults in view. However, infants and children and the "incapacitated" were not excluded. Thomas M. Finn, *The Early Christian Baptism and the Catechumenate: West and East Syria* (Minnesota: The Liturgical Press, 1992), 14- 15

[44] Baby Varghese, *Baptism and Chrismation in the Syriac Tradition* (Kottayam: SEERI), 28.

the baptised has the full right to partake of the "celestial banquet."[45]

Theologically, the faith that constitutes the very life of the Church and of her members is of a greater degree and essence than that of personal faith—regardless of children or adults. Baptism depends on Christ's faith, and the gift of his faith is the true grace. This is based on the biblical injunction that "as many of you as were baptized into Christ have clothed yourselves with Christ" (Gal. 3:27).[46]

Baptismal Theology and Children in Western Thought

Augustine's thesis on sin and children—that stands juxtaposed to the Eastern theology, especially his theology of baptism—is a strong pointer to his theology of childhood. Augustine claims that infants are born sinful and express sinful tendencies, but recognises that they are physically unable to sin due to their state of "non-innocence" and thus are not yet guilty of specific sins. Yet, they are affected by the original sin and, therefore, not born innocent. He argues:

> Even infants show sinful tendencies; Adam's transgressions, which implant in his progeny an alien sin, account for these tendencies; and Baptism remedies these damnable tendencies and should be confessed as early as possible. [47]

Both Eastern and Western theological thoughts insist on baptism as a means of God's grace without which the "original sin" that children seem to have inherited cannot be blotted out. Can we not, then, understand the grace of God outside these sacraments,

---

[45] Baby Varghese, *Baptism and Chrismation,...*, 66-67.

[46] Alexander Schmemann, *Of Water and the Spirit* (Crestwood, NY: St. Vladimir's Seminary Press, 1995), 66- 69.

[47] Martha Ellen Stortz, "'Where or When Was Your Servant Innocent?': Augustine on Childhood" in *The Child in Christian Thought*, edited by Marcia J. Bunge, 78- 102.

more specifically in the context of children who are unduly dragged into the discourses of the adult world?

Children, Liberation Theology and Childhood Studies

Within liberation theology, feminist movements and corresponding theologies have taken up children's concern with greater sensitivity. To a great extent, "Feminist maternal theology" has tried to respond to the need for representing children.[48] The issues of motherhood, family and social justice are the three important fields that feminist theologians have explored with regard to children issues. Nonetheless, only those theologies that represent children's theophonic "still small voices" can radicalise the movement.

Liberation theologies in India like Dalit theology, tribal theology, feminist theology, eco-theology, etc., have carried with them many of the metanarratives that have come in the baggage of the Latin American liberation theology. They have projected conventional paradigms like the anthropocentric approach, patriarchal notions, adult discourses and so on. Of late, even in the process of divesting theologies of these biased paradigms, the unique questions of children's suppression have not been adequately addressed. Children need emancipation from a world chiefly designed for adult aspirations. Ideologically, liberation theologies have exhibited a greater bend to oppressive issues. Therefore, the issue of child labour would soon get due attention. [49]

---

[48] The Feminist Maternal theology suggests asking not only how fresh understanding of children might influence motherhood but also how contemporary experiences of mothering shape understanding of children. Bonnie J. Miller- McLemore, "'Let the Children Come' Revisited: Contemporary Feminist Theologians on Children" in *The Child in Christian Thought*, edited by Marcia J. Bunge..., 450- 455. Also by McLemore, "Children and Religion in the Public Square," ..., 385- 410.

[49] Naomi Steinberg, "1 Samuel 1, the United Nations Convention on the Rights of Children, and 'The Best Interests of the Child".

Theologies of "childhood" and "Child Theology Movement" within Christian theology have emphasised the need to incorporate children's concerns and their voices. This movement brings together scholars from disciplines spanning theology, anthropology and ethical issues.[50] In these discourses, children are removed from the traditional theological frameworks that have either excluded or belittled them and are placed in the midst of theological discourses as interpretative voices in the light of the values of God's reign. However, the issue of labouring children has not got its due attention in these theologies as yet.

Labour *in the Hebrew Scripture*

The biblical instances that provide the bases for conceptual analysis of labour are, obviously, undergirded by the adult-labouring experience. Methodologically, adult experiences cannot represent the labouring children's plight.

The word "labour" can incorporate a plethora of divine and human activities ranging from creative activity of God to people working for wages, the generation of energy for useful purposes

---

[50] The recently evolving "Child Theology Movement" has emphasized the need to incorporate children's concerns and their voices. This movement brings together scholars from disciplines spanning theology, anthropology, and ethical issues. The children, in these discourses, are removed from the traditional theological frameworks that have either excluded or belittled them, and are placed "in the midst" of theological discourses as interpretative voices in the light of the values of God's reign. However, the issues of labouring children have not got adequate attention in these theologies as yet. For a detailed explanation and demonstrated works see, http://www. childtheology.org . Also see Marcia J. Bunge, ed., *The Child in Christian Thought* (Michigan/ Cambridge: William B. Eerdmans Publishing Company); *JJ* 86/4 (October 2006)- This is a Special issue on "Religion and Childhood Studies"; John Wall, "Human Rights in Light of Children: A Christian Childist Perspective," *JPT* 17/1 (2007): 54- 67. Also, *Dharma Deepika* 12/2 (Issue 28, July-Dec. 2008); Jesudason B. Jeyaray Ed. *Children at Risk: Issues and Challenges* (Delhi/Banglore: ISPCK/CFCD, 2009)

and becoming co-creators with God in the effort to refining God's will in the creation. The Hebrew noun *Yegia* can denote "toil" or "work", especially its burdensome nature (Gen. 3:17, 31:42; Job 39:11, 16). Although most often it meant the "fruit of the toil", it is but "the result for which one labored."[51] The noun *Amal* denotes ideas like "a difficult labour" (Eccles. 1:3), "the whole life-enterprise as a laborious task" (occurs time and again in Eccles. and Ps. 90:10), "product or fruit of labor" and so on. This is also used to describe Israel's slave labour in Egypt (Deut. 26:7). It expresses Israel's similar state at the hand of its enemies (Judg. 10: 6). It is also used to explain the works of the wicked, especially the unjust treatment they meted out to the innocent through their corrupt power (Ps. 94: 20-21). It is in such an "oppressive state" that God denounces decrees that produce oppression (Isa. 10: 1).[52] In both the cases, it is not slogging for the sake of slogging but to partake in God's creative economy and to share the fruit of labour. Wherever there is an unjust defining of this concept, God comes to the rescue and liberation of the sufferer.

Resources of Labour as a Means of Life for All

An assortment of the ensuing themes from the above-mentioned terms enriches our understanding of the concept of work and labour. This offers space for multiple possibilities in the matter of their explanation and their relevance to our situation. Firstly, divine activity (work) and human activity (work) seem to be on different levels. While God's activity is "essentially creative", human activities reproduce towards refinement according to the

---

[51] David L. Thompson, "Yg", *NIDOTTE,* edited by William A. VanGemeren, vol 2 (Grand Rapids, Michigan: Zondervan Publishing House, 1997), 400-02.

[52] David Thomson, "Amal," *NIDOTTE,* edited by William A. VanGemeren, vol 3 (Grand Rapids, Michigan: Zondervan Publishing House, 1997), 435.

need of the society. Human activity is presented as a skill from Lord's blessings and teachings (Isa. 28: 23-29). The reflection of God's work in human work presupposes the image of God in human beings. Secondly, human labour is meant to bring about blessings to the community. A society in which people enjoy the opportunities and rewards of work is an ideal condition.

The Image of God and Labour

Imago Dei assists our attempt towards an organic relationship between the creative activity of work and the fruit of the work as divinely purposed. It represents the natural relationship between God's creative and liberative work, between material and spiritual needs of people and the need for labour and rest (Deut. 5:13). While, in the Hebrew Scripture, work and labour are "necessary and indeed God-appointed", prophetic anger arose when the slaves were not remunerated with suitable wages (Jer. 22:13). Another form of remuneration was rest. The fourth commandment of the Decalogue attests to this form of remuneration in the form of rest on Sabbath. The Jubilee motif, a mechanism to prevent slavery and to preserve the socioeconomic fabric, proclaims the release of powerless bonded slaves and labourers from their debt to and bondage from the masters (Exod. 21; 23:1-12; Lev. 26:35, 40 and 43). The theology of Sabbath proposes every human being to be the "imitation of God" (*imitatio Dei*) and participate in God's creative activities and in rest. Rest, which is a "divine gift of freedom from the labors of human existence"[53], signifies liberation from unethical and exploitative work situations. The motivating power for the liberative aspect of labour is the prophetic vision of a time when people "shall not labour in vain" (Isa. 65:23).

---

[53] Gerhard F. Hasel, "Sabbath," *ABD* vol. 5, edited by David Noel Freedman (New York: Doubleday, 1997, 1992), 849- 856

Missionally, as Douglas Meeks observes, God calls humans into partnership with God's creative and liberative work.[54] Therefore, *Imago Dei* becomes a powerful model to look up to.

Labour in New Testament Epistles: Is *Imitatio Dei* Misrepresented?

The *Haustafel* (Col. 3:22, 4: 1; Eph. 6: 5-9; 1 Tim. 6; 1 Peter 2:18-25) highlights the social structure of the early Christian community and emphasises the type of relationship between the slave-owner and the slaves. 1 Peter 2:18-25 deals with the submission of slaves to both kind and harsh masters. Here a work ethic is introduced as a rationale to justify the unquestionable authority of masters and subordination of slaves. The abused slave is projected as a symbol of 'imitation of Christ' and the suffering of the community is justified for the sake of their faith. However, the abuse of slaves (both male and female) could be physical including sexual exploitation. However, a proverb in the Greco-Roman milieu of early Christianity captured another negative dimension of the slave-master relationship. It said: "You have as many enemies as you have slaves."[55]

In James 5:1-6, the writer slams a prophetic warning at the hedonistic attitude exhibited in the Church, especially in its approach to the working class. The cries of the unpaid wagers are unequivocally directed towards condemning the rich, for such a cry is a reminder that wealthy people amass various commodities and so hold back to themselves not only what is supposed to be

---

[54] Douglas M Meeks, *God the Economist: The Doctrine of God and Political Economy* (Mineapolis: Fortress Press, 1989), 137.

[55] Seneca, *Epistle* 47.5, as cited by Carolyn Osiek in, "Female Slaves, *Porneia*, and the Limits of Obedience," in *Early Christian Families in Context. An Interdisciplinary Dialogue*, edited by David L. Balch and Carolyn Osiek (Grand Rapids: William B. Eerdmans Publishing Company, 2003), 272.

shared with the poor, but also what is actually due to the wagers. This cry may be the combination of the pain related to hunger and the desire that God should act to vindicate them.[56]

The so-understood "nonresistance of the righteous" (v. 6) to the threat of persecution needs appropriate evaluation.[57] What often passes off as a "non-resistant group" has underlying it such an ethos of long periods of restraint on resistance. In one sense, the oppressed has helplessly assimilated this "non-resistant" culture.[58] Especially children with ravished innocence and no knowledge of any system of resistance would all the more be the ones needing the voice and awareness to resist. Particularly, in an unorganised work situation, resistance is opposed with brutal force. Workers are silent witnesses to their own suffering. An

---

[56] The above discussed situation emerged in a situation where (1) farming and commerce were linked, the landowners could bring their food directly to market and dominate the price structure with volume production; (2) lack of capital prevented the small farmer from expanding his holding and upgrading one's equipment; (3) in time of drought and famine, the large landowner had more resources on which to call and could hoard his produce or, when market forces operated to his advantage, sell at inflated prices. By contrast, the small farmer had no reserves and was driven either to sell out to the magnate or to take a loan at high interest rates, and with the threat of expropriation for the default of payment a real one; and (4) the tendency was for the rural independent to be squeezed out of business and to become a wage earner or tenant farmer or worker in the employ of his feudal master. Martin, Ralph P., "James," *WBC*, vol. 48, edited by David A. Hubbard and Glenn W. Barker (Dallas, Texas: Word Books, Publisher, 1998), 174. Also see, Christoph Stuckelberger, *Global Trade Ethics: An Illustrated Overview* (Geneva: WCC Publications, 2002), 16.

[57] Martin, Ralph P., "James,"…, 174.

[58] Bill Ashcroft, Gareth Griffiths and Helen Tiffin, *Key Concepts in Post-Colonial Studies* (London and New York: Routledge, 2004), 139-141.

earlier Christian tradition even has it that a slave or a servant is not eligible to bear witness to an incident or a wrongdoing.[59]

Paul has an analysis of "covetousness" that may well serve as a rubric under which James' indictments are to be placed. This can also be best rendered as "acquisitiveness." Here, Paul's remark is tantamount to idolatry (Col. 3:5). The outlook that our possessions are an end in themselves is challenged here resonating Mathew's words, "You cannot serve God and wealth" (Matt 6:24).[60]

Jesus and Labour Movement

Jesus had a large following, a majority of whom belonged to the labouring class (Matt. 4:25; Mark 5:21, 6:34, 9:15; Luke. 6:17, 9:37; John. 7:31, 8:2, 12:9). Jesus' upbringing in a labour-class family would have helped him to take up the cause of the labouring section of Herodian Palestine. This class was taxed and collected rent from for the use of land.[61] The influence of a very small population over the labour-force-centred society had already produced mass uprisings.[62] Jesus' social position in his times gave him an opportunity to advocate the cause of the labouring class in the form of "brokering."[63] Therefore, Jesus died the death of an

---

[59] As mentioned by St. Basil. See, Blomfield Jackson, translated with notes, *The Treatise De Spiritu Sancto: The Nine Homilies of the Hexaemeron and the Letters of St. Basil the Great Archbishop of Caesarea*, vol. 8 *NPNF*, 2ⁿᵈ series (Grand Rapids, Michigan: Wm. B. Eerdmans Publishing Company, 1955), 190-191. (Hereafter, *"The Treatise De Spiritu Sancto"*).

[60] Martin, Ralph P., "James".

[61] David Fiensy, "Leaders of Mass Movements and the Leader of the Jesus Movement," *JSNT* 74 (1999): 4-6.

[62] Fiensy presents two lists of Mass Movements that emerged at various periods in the Roman Empire and in Palestine. They were political and prophetic in nature. David Fiensy, "Leaders of Mass Movements and the Leader of the Jesus Movement,"..., 11-13.

[63] David Fiensy, "Leaders of Mass Movements and the Leader of the Jesus Movement,"..., 14-27.

"insurrectionist." Out of the creative tension of negotiating, Jesus worked out an emancipatory situation for the labouring class of his times.

Labour in Christian Theology

From the time of the early teachers of the Church to the time of present theological-anthropologists, discussions on work and labour have received sizeable attention. However, the growth of industrial technology and capitalism, especially in Europe, has shifted the emphasis from the labour force to the capital-oriented activities largely favouring the dominant class, the capitalists. Such dominant discourses have been attributed to the colonial form of Christianity. In the present era, globalisation has borne the traits of capitalism and colonialism—with a difference! Globalisation, with greater technological invention, intervention and interference, disclaims the traditional discourses on labour. Here, too, our theologies have responded to these economic processes as either "development" or "decline." Moreover, the concept of "economy", which earlier meant "household as the site of economy of God to meet the necessities of life", has metamorphosised, rather narrowly, referring autonomously to profit-oriented market management. In all these themes, there is a clear invisibility of the children in the labour force in a majority of theological discourses. The examination in the following sections attempts to bring to the fore, to put it in the words of Wielenga, "the class of non-owners."[64] It is in this context that thoughts span the worth of the labouring child as an image of God and a dignified citizen.

---

[64] Bastian Wielenga, *Biblical Perspectives on Labour* (Madurai: Tamil Nadu Theological Seminary, 1982), 7.

Work and Slavery: Reflections from Early Teachers

The early Christian literature indicates the presence of child-slaves in the households. Over and against the inculcation of Christian ethic into the New Testament household codes, the early Christians adapted to Greco-Roman hierarchical household management including keeping child-slaves. Justin the Martyr comments that the authorities "dragged to torture also our domestic slaves… either children or women and by dreadful torments forced them to admit those incredible actions."[65] With such infrequent discourses on child-slaves, frameworks for understanding children could be drawn only from the general teachings of early teachers on work, slavery and freedom.

In their treatises, teachers like Ambrose, John Chrysostom, Gregory of Nyssa and Basil uphold the basic equality and freedom of all human beings—that slaves are no less humans and that slaves are subject to passion. Slavery was one of the most important social questions that the *Didache* and the teachers had to respond to.

However, the teachers were permeated by the tendency of the age and stopped short of condemning slavery as contrary to human dignity. It seemed to the teachers that slavery was an economic necessity, or a product of war, or consequence of sin, and one of the fundamental institutions of the social order, which the Church did not contemplate to destroy. Rather they sought to justify it for the "glory of God."[66] Basil's view of slavery is grounded in Aristotle's position for an inevitable stratification of

---

[65] Justin [2 *Apology 12. 4*] as quoted by J. Albert Harrill, "The Domestic Enemy: A Moral Portrait of Household Slaves in Early Christian Apologies and Martyrdoms," in edited by David L. Balch and Carolyn Osiek (Grand Rapids: William B. Eerdmans Publishing Company, 2003), 245.

[66] Peter C. Phan, *Social Thought* (Wilmington, Delaware: Michael Glazier, Inc., 1984), 34.

human society based on the needs and works of human beings, and therefore, *Natural*. Basil (as Aristotle) sees the advantage to the weak slave having a powerful protector; and this, no doubt, is the point of view from which "slavery can be best apologized."[67] He mentions that slaves could not stand before the judge to witness an event. In his letter to Simplicia "the Heretic", Basil states:

> [Slaves] at the very birth... are condemned to knife. How can their mind be right when their feet are awry? They are chaste because of the knife, and it is no credit to them. They are lecherous to no purpose, of their own **natural** vileness. These are not the witnesses who shall stand in the judgment but rather the eyes of the just and the eyesight of the perfect, of all who are then to see with their eyes what they now see with their understanding. [68]

---

[67] Based on Aristotelian *Natural* thesis, Basil proposes two theological presuppositions. Firstly, concerning our relation to god, all created beings are naturally in a condition of subservience to the Creator. Secondly, concerning our relationship to one another, slavery is not of nature, but of intended by nature to be a slave, and for whom such a condition is expedient and right. Furthering these thoughts, he says that it is not only necessary, but expedient that some should rule, and others be ruled, as they are marked out for subjection since birth. Where, then, there is such a difference between soul and body, or between men and animals (as in the case of those whose business is it to use their body, and who can do nothing better) the lowest sort are by nature slaves, and it is better for them, as for all inferiors, that they should be under the rule of a master...It is clear, then, that some men are by nature free and others slaves, and that for these latter slavery is both expedient and right." Book 1, Sec. 5). Here by *Nature* seems to be meant something like Basil's "lack of intelligence" and that which makes it "profitable" for one man to be the chattel (cattle) of another. "Chapter XX: Against those who maintain that the spirit is in the rank neither of a servant nor of a master but in that of the free", *The Treatise De Spiritu Sancto...*, 32n.

[68] "Letter CXV: To the Heretic Simplicia," *The Treatise De Spiritu Sancto...*, 190-191. (*Emphasis mine*).

At the same time, it was in the age of Basil that "the language of the Fathers assumes a bolder tone." In one of the correspondences of Gregory of Nazianzen, we find him referring to a case where a slave had been made bishop over a small Christian community in the desert.[69]

While Clement and Origen advocated treating slaves as equals, Tertullian and Jerome were not too kind to slaves. Tertullian compared demons to rebellious slaves, and Jerome accused them of being money grabbers and of spreading scandals. The Council of Ganga in 340 C.E. decreed: "If anyone teaches a slave, under pretext of piety, to despise his [sic] master [sic], to forsake his service, not to serve him with good will and all respect, let him be anathema" (Canon 3).[70] Therefore, one can admire their teachings on human worth and, at the same time, find them wanting on practical grounds.

Similar to Basil's position was that of John Chrysostom. Chrysostom explains how Paul's non-condemnation of slavery on the ground that its existence, with that of Christian liberty, was a greater moral triumph than its abolition.[71] To put it in the words of Chrysostom,

> For this reason also, from the beginning, God tied the man
> to labour, not for the purpose of punishing or chastising, but

---

[69] *The Treatise De Spiritu Sancto…*,190n

[70] Peter C. Phan, *Social Thought…*, 34.

[71] Even so late as the sixth century, the legislation of Justinian, though protective, supposed no natural liberty. We must not therefore be surprised at not finding in a Father of the fourth century an anticipation of a later development of Christian sentiment. The Christian lady, Simplicia (190n) to whom he belonged endeavored to assert her right of ownership, for which she was severely rebuked by Basil. After Basil's death she again claimed the slave, whereupon Gregory addressed her a letter of grave remonstrance at her unchristian desire to recall his brother bishop from his sphere of duty. Philip Schaff, *NPNF* Vol IX, 190.

for amendment and education. When Adam lived an unlabourious life, he fell from the paradise, but when the apostle laboured abundantly, and toiled hard, and said, 'In labour and travail, working night and day' then he was taken up into paradise, and ascended to the third heaven... Let us not then despise labour; let us not despise work; for before the kingdom of heaven, we receive the greatest recompense from thence, deriving pleasure from that circumstance; and not pleasure alone, but what is greater than pleasure, the purest health.[72]

Medieval Church on Work and Labour

Bastian Wielenga, in his survey of Christian response to Capitalism, identifies three characteristic responses to the development of capitalism. While the medieval church and the Reformation considered any interest in capitalism as "usury and therefore mortal sin", the Reformation, especially through Martin Luther, saw mammon at the core of capitalism. Although one could notice a prophetic move in Luther's critique, Wielenga observes conformity to a traditional medieval view that took feudal society as an unproblematic norm. At best, the Church could appeal to the business world for charity towards the poor. Wielenga calls this a 'Conservative Protest.' Also, there were radical protests and uprisings in the Reformation-Muentzer and Peasants ordeal and particularly in the English Revolution (1640-1660). The Puritan radicals and revolutionary Baptists called for sorting out values on an egalitarian basis. The spirit of 'Revolutionary Protests'—as Wielenga calls it—could be seen in the German peasants and English Diggers who were "crucified in bloody repression." [73]

---

[72] *Saint Chrysostom: On the Priesthood; Ascetic Treatises; Select Homilies and Letters; Homilies on the Statutes,* vol 9 of *NPNF,* edited by Philip Schaff (Grand Rapids, Michigan: Wm. B. Eerdmans Publishing Company, 1956), 352- 353.

[73] Bastian Wielenga, *Labour- Serving God or Mammon?* (Delhi: ISPCK, 1987), 22- 28.

Work, Labour and Capitalism in Protestantism

The Reformation tradition, especially from Calvinist undertakings, suggests an understanding of the "secular work" as "divine" and exploration of possibilities of work (business) where one's talents could be adequately used. Max Weber's thesis is that capitalism, and consequently the very structure of modern Western society, is a product of Protestantism. Therefore, it was a "sociological type" of religious explanation that promoted a form of work culture. This had brought the theory of Predestination, leaving many confused about whether they were 'elected' or not. So one felt it necessary to "prove" one's worth in this life through strong entrepreneurship and ascetic living. "Choosing a less gainful way would be a refusal to be God's steward." To be enterprising was divine. It fostered "the habit of saving for investment as providing a good conscience in paying low wages" for the hard work forced on the poor.[74]

Summing up the churches' response to the rise of capitalism with Industrial Revolution, Andre Biele observes that the most damaging aspect of the Industrial Revolution was— and is—the proletarianisation of the ever-growing human masses that flocked into industrial zones in search of employment. This phenomenon is the annihilation of the fundamental human character as the image of God and "devitalizes" and "depersonalizes" the proletariats. Generally, neither of the denominational groups made

---

[74] Weber "finds in the Lutheran state church a stagnant bureaucratic state apparatus that was 'peculiar to feudalism and conservatism, the officers' core and feudal civil service' but was penetrating into the middle class Germany rendering it impotent to bring the kind of political economic revolution necessary to Germany into a national power that would rival Anglo-America". In his 1920 version, Weber moves from a cultural specific critique to a civilizational analysis where Catholicism and other world religions are included. William H. Swatos, Jr. and Peter Kivisto, "Max Weber as 'Christian Sociologist'," *JSSR*, 30 (1991), 357.

common cause with the working classes in their struggle to improve status and general position in society with exceptions in the Catholic group of the French Christian socialists and the Protestant Christian socialists in England in the 19th century.[75]

Modern Theologians' Views on Labour

Karl Barth presents a representative thought of modern theologians on labour and capitalism. He sees counter-movements in God's commands at humanity's behest. However, Christianity has not responded in time to its context. He says:

> The Christian community has undoubtedly been too late in seeing this in face of the modern capitalistic development of the labour process, and it cannot escape some measure of responsibility for the injustice characteristic of this development.... The main task of Christianity in the West is ... to assert the command of God in the face of [capitalism], and to keep to the 'left' in opposition to its champions, i.e., to confess that it is fundamentally on the side of the victims of this disorder and to espouse their cause. [76]

When "evil is socialized, salvation [too] must be socialized," says Walter Rauschenbusch.[77] In the process of sharing the resources, the rich have treated some as slaves. Quoting Fichte, Rauschenbusch says, "Whoever treats another as slave, becomes a slave" and adds that "whoever treats the slave as a child of God becomes a child of God and learns to know God."[78] However, he

---

[75] Andre Bieler, "Gradual Awareness of Social, Economic Problem (1750-1900)," in *Separation Without Hope? Essays on the Relation between the Church and the Poor During the Industrial Revolution and the Western Colonial Expansion,* edited by Julio de Santa Ana (Geneva: World Council of Churches, 1978), 3- 29.

[76] Karl Barth, *Church Dogmatics* III/4, translated by G. W. Bromiley and R. J. Ehrlich (Edinburgh: T & T Clarke, 1960), 544.

[77] Walter Rauschenbusch, *The Social Principles of Jesus* (New York: Association Press, 1927), 163.

[78] Walter Rauschenbusch, *The Social Principles of Jesus...,* 14

does not critique the undergirding principles of capitalism and unequal sharing of wealth and the consequent hierarchy.

Some Recent Theological-Ethical Discourses on Labour

Three important works of the recent past—Pope John Paul II's Encyclical Letter *Laborem Exercens* (1981),[79] Bastian Wielenga's *Biblical Perspectives on Labour* and Douglas Meeks's *God the Economist* (1989)[80]—have presented theological discourses on labour. While the Pope presents a "subjective dimension of Work"[81] based on Christology, Meeks' discourse is modeled on the function of the Trinity. Wielenga culls out the liberative aspect of God's economy for a "critical and political" engagement.

In his treatise on labour, Pope John Paul II proposes (a) priority of labour over capital in harmony with the doctrine of creation; (b) principles of relation in employment practices, impersonal corporations and the functions and limits of trade unions, specifically agricultural and migrant workers as finer aspects of Marxism; and (c) spirituality of work as founded upon Christianity, based on the Christological theme—Christ, the man of work who sweat and toiled. [82] He, however, prefers "to be in

---

[79] This discourse was presented to commemorate the ninetieth anniversary of *Rerum Novarum* of Pope Leo XIII. See, *Pope John Paul II: Encyclicals* (Trivandrum: Carmel International Publishing House, 2005), 945-1010.

[80] Douglas M Meeks, *God the Economist...*, 127-155.

[81] For commentaries on *Labourem Exercens*, see Pontifical Council for Justice and Peace, *Work as Key to the Social Question: The Great Social and Economic Transformations and the Subjective Dimension of Work*, (Vatican City: Libreria Editrice Vaticana, 2002). Also, see Gabriele Dietrich's comments on *Labourem Exercens* in the chapter, "Emerging Feminist and Ecological Concerns in Asia," in her *A New Thing on Earth: Hopes and Fears Facing Feminist Theology* (Delhi/ Madurai: ISPCK/ TTS, 2001), 161- 166.

[82] Monika K. Hellwig, "Labourem Exercens," in *MCE* edited by Michael Glazier and Monika K. Hellwig (Bangalore: Claritan Publications, 1992), 489.

the organic connection" with the Church's conventional dualism of theology and political economy where the "scientific analysis" of human crises is not by the Church.[83] He also generalises and spiritualises the violation of dignity through oppressed labour as the "Cross" — as in union with the Christ crucified. However, what is intriguing is his stance on "enduring" the hardship ("cross which the world and the flesh inflict upon those who pursue peace and justice") of labour one is called upon to perform. He masks it as "work in union with Christ crucified for us..." and as collaboration "with the Son of God for the redemption of humanity."[84]

Very few scholars in and around India have contextually explicated the biblical and theological precepts of labour. Of them, the one who profoundly combines the biblical precepts of labour and our social context is Bastiaan Wielenga (See his works, such as *Labour:Serving God or Mammon?* and *Biblical Perspectives on Labour).* Basing his analysis on a class-ridden society, Wielenga says that "the Bible can speak to us concretely only if we are ready to go into an analysis of our own situation."[85] While the Bible can give a sense of direction to a situation, one's understanding of one's own context serves as a crucial lead to respond to any unethical situation. Kingdom concerns could be made tangible to the deserving by understanding the political situation and by involving oneself in a sustained political struggle and in the affairs of society and community.[86] According to his analysis of Christian history, Christianity's promotion of the capitalist ideology was the greatest shortcoming in the Churches' approach. By succumbing

---

[83] *Pope John Paul II: Encyclicals...,* 949

[84] *Pope John Paul II: Encyclicals...,* 1002- 1007

[85] Bastian Wielenga, *Biblical Perspectives on Labour...,*4.

[86] Bastian Wielenga, *Biblical Perspectives on Labour...,*117

to the capitalist's lure, the Church called the business as "divine calling" and carried "the cross of exploitation."[87]

Douglas Meeks' *God the Economist* has a specific task of rescuing economic philosophy from popular market connotations. He attempts to reinstate the deeper biblical understanding of the "economy" of God as of the "oikos" (the world as a "household"), in which God is the economist who conceptualises the household there is always enough to go around.

In the discourse on "God and Work", the concept of property is inclusive, where all have a right in the sharing of goods (though Meeks does not deny the importance of some exclusive property rights!) just as each person of the Trinity shares its substance with the others. Need, which is ambiguously presented in our culture as systematically created consumer want, is understood in the Trinitarian perspective as fulfillable without scarcity in the *oikos* of God. Firstly, the Trinity engages in *distinctive personal work* just as each person of the Trinity contributes to the divine economy; secondly, it engages in *cooperative work* just as the members of the Trinity do—no member works in isolation; thirdly, it is the *equalitarian work* of the Trinity, where the work of no one is elevated above that of the other. In the process, it breaks down hierarchies and negates any dominant power. Fourthly, "it is the integration of the Triune community's work through *self-giving* love of each other. The work of each is done for the life of the community."[88]

In conclusion, we are confronted with a common thread of disadvantage that runs through the discouses on labour: the clear absence of discourses from the point of view of children and child labourers/workers/slaves in Christian theology. This has devoid us of a clear point of reference from which we theologically address

---

[87] Bastian Wielenga, *Biblical Perspectives on Labour...*,17- 29.

[88] Douglas M Meeks, *God the Economist...*, 132- 134.

the groans of labouring children. This has serious ramifications on the identity of child labourers in the Church and society. All the more detrimental is the negative picturing of their place and role, which can reinstate child labour in an unapologising manner as we see in the case of Basil's discourse. Ironically, toeing of the similar line by our theologies that claim to be liberative has blinded our theologies to the horrific plight of child labourers. Only the victims know better the limitations of such ideologies and theologies while being unaware that churches and theologies can take their sides as an embedded factor in their calling and commitment. Nevertheless, also clearly visible in our discussion are the signs of hope and reclamation to move towards restoration of fullness of life and position to children. These liberative elements could be emphasised along with highlighting the positive picture of children in our traditions. Therefore, agencies claiming the "image of God" and emancipation of children would co-create with God a conscientious location for those children who seek representation and recognition. The following chapter attempts to see how our theological lenses could be sharpened and widened to analyse this liberative identity and recognition that could be worked out for the labouring children in the intriguing Indian socio-political, economic and cultural scenario. This compels theology to play the role of a monitoring agency.

CHAPTER 3

Child Labour and Liberation Theology in India: A Case of Dalit Theology

This chapter interrogates the absence of the concept of child labour in the discursive body of theological thought in India, especially in the liberation theologies in India. While the socio-cultural location of these children is generally the same as those that liberation theology seeks to resist and liberate, it is an irony that the circumstances that determine child labourers' identity are not given adequate consideration in Dalit, tribal and feminist liberation discourses. In addition, even if one demands an empirical knowledge to substantiate the inadequacy of liberation theology in India, the need for incorporating the plight of child labourers is pressing, with around 75 per cent of child labourers belonging to Dalit and other subaltern sections of our society. This highlights how our theologies have uncritically inherited the adult-bias in their theological methodologies. Therefore, addressing these concerns, especially of child labourers, would broaden the horizons of our theological praxis.

Here, the critical insights from postcolonial criticism—as an analytical tool—comes to play by engaging in liberation theologies in India to trace their trajectories to interrogate those factors that have created dominant and subordinate narratives leading to the "non- presence" of child labourers. It also promotes the inclusion of labouring children as significant theological category through formulating some hermeneutical keys to understanding the living situation of child labourers.

Advocating the cause of child labourers in theological conversation has immense scope and consequence. The advocacy method along with the interventionist skill of postcolonial criticism advances the claims of child labourers for a rightful hearing of their pathetic stories and establishes an agential significance of their presence for doing theology of the underside. Here, I will dwell on Sathianathan Clarke's proposal of advocacy function of theology employable towards constructing a discourse. Clarke, in his *Dalits and Christianity,* says that:

> The critical role of theology moves beyond mere astute diagnosis of the content; it also ascertains what is missing from the theological discourse. It is thus crucial to locate, recover and validate critique-based voices that are contesting the content and the process of the dominant and dominating religious discourse... The role of theology involves taking on the task of advocating for the marginalized so that they will be seen and heard within the reflective and dialogical process of theologizing. Theology thus puts into circulation oppositional, discordant and anomalous voices that are generally suppressed or evicted.[1]

Mapping Liberation Theology: Child Labourer in the Body of God

Liberation theology in India characterises a new awakening in Indian Christian theology alongside the movements that took up the causes of Dalits, tribals, women and the environment. It has also, to a certain extent, taken people's movements as theological tools and has developed with the thrust on improved social status, for a greater sense of personal dignity and self-respect, for freedom

---

[1] Sathianathan Clarke, *Dalits and Christianity: Subaltern Religion and Liberation Theology in India,* (Delhi: Oxford University Press, 1998), 20.

from bondage to oppressive landowners, for rightful identity as images of God, for a rightful place in the Body of God and for revealing the understanding that God in Jesus Christ identifies with the pathos of the oppressed.

The different versions of liberation theologies in India exhibit some of the typical characteristics of the liberation theology of Latin America. While "liberation" is the overarching objective in both these forms, a theology such as Dalit theology specifically addresses the predicaments of the wronged-against by caste-based manoeuvres. Tribal theologies retrieve the lost tradition of varieties of tribal spiritualities that are closely linked with land and creation, emphasising the communitarian aspect of sharing and living. In its earliest forms, liberation theology focused on class- and caste-based discrimination and proposed a hermeneutical circle that began with the experience of the oppressed poor. Similar to the concerns of the Latin American liberation theology, the emergence of Dalit liberation has its roots in the labour movement, especially focusing on landless labourers and small-scale farmers.[2] Taking cues from early liberation theology, Dalit theology gives space for the identity of the working class. Feminist theologies on their own have raised the bar to challenge the embedded patriarchal notions of these theologies.

With a methodological intent, these variants of liberation theologies initiated the objectives of revision and reformulation of the elitist Indian Christian Theology by dissenting and defying the traditional metaphysical speculations that did not interface with the marginalised majority within the Indian Church. The earlier theologies coming from the West or elsewhere did not include Dalitness or tribalness in their discourse, and therefore, theologies were "ineffective." Such theologies were not able to

---

[2] George Mathew Nalunnakkal, *Green Liberation: Towards an Integral Ecotheology* (Delhi: IPSCK/NCCI, 1999), xvii.

kindle sympathetic thoughts towards subaltern concerns for the reason that they were "overly academic, abstract and ahistorical" and, therefore, "naturally failed" to respond to the real situation.[3] In the words of Clarke, "Indian-Christian theology [was] non-dialogical and non-representative of the symbolic interaction of the whole community."[4] It was "an instrument of ideological co-option rather than human liberation."[5]

Dalit theology has evolved in two ways: firstly, as a resistance of the Dalits to counter the reach of dominant theologies, and secondly, as a creative construction to circulate themes of Dalits' experience of the Divine.[6] As a resistance movement to the non-participatory approach of theologies, theologians like Arvind P. Nirmal, James Massey, M.E. Prabhakar, M. Azariah, K. Wilson, V. Devasahayam and F.J. Balasundaram challenged the Brahmanic tradition within the Church and highlighted the rich cultural and religious experience of the Dalits who were ignored for a long time. This "methodological exclusivism",[7] while restricting the liberative sustenance through collaborations, also meant a creative

---

[3] James Massey and T. K. John, "Concept Paper: Centre for Dalit/ Subaltern Studies," in *Frontiers in Dalit Hermeneutics*, edited by James Massey, and Samson Prabhakar (Bangalore/Delhi: BTESSC-SATHRI/ CDSS, 2005), 287- 288.

[4] Sathianathan Clarke, *Dalits and Christianity: Subaltern Religion and Liberation Theology in India* (Delhi: Oxford University Press, 1998), 35.

[5] Sathianathan Clarke, *Dalits and Christianity...*, 41.

[6] Sathianathan Clarke, "Dalit Theology" in *Dictionary of Third World Theologies*, edited by Virginia Fabella and R. S. Sugirtharajah (Maryknoll, New York: Orbis Books, 2000) 64- 65.

[7] Arvind P. Nirmal, "Towards a Christian Dalit Theology,' in *A Reader in Dalit Theology*, edited by Arvind P. Nirmal (Madras: GURUKUL, 1991), 58- 59. On the same issue see, V. Devasahayam, "Doing Dalit Theology: Basic Assumptions," in *Frontiers of Dalit Theology*, edited by V. Devasahayam (Madras: ISPCK/ GURUKUL, 1997), 281- 282; V Devasahayam, "The Nature of Dalit Theology as Counter Ideology" in *Frontiers of Dalit Theology...*, 53.

eruption of remedial formulations from within without being overly conforming to outside viewpoints. Progressive Dalit thinkers like K. Wilson and Balasundaram realised the need for interconnectedness of liberative resources and the inclusive temperament of the Dalit theology.[8] These formulations lay bare the struggle for greater self-identity of Dalits and greater emphases on working the broader framework of Dalit theology to develop liberative models from ingenious sources.[9]

For theologising the same, Dalit hermeneutics derives principles from the sociology of Knowledge. Dalit realities/ experiences and therefore the Dalit consciousness are essentially learnt in a social matrix, which has epistemic significance. Dalit theology and hermeneutics share a converging point since both are not innocent methods, but struggle to establish justice with their inherent ideological commitments.[10]

As a creative constructive stance, feminist theological movement within the Dalit theology highlighted—apart from the commonly perceived Dalit pathos[11]—a type of methodological exclusivity of the gender-stereotype in theological discourse and sought to rectify it by interfacing theological discourse and women's movements.[12] Monica Melancthon explains how the

---

[8] Sathianathan Clarke, *Dalits and Christianity...*, 41.

[9] Despite claims of exclusive methodological stance, Arvind Nirmal seems to be open to such efforts. See Arvind P. Nirmal, "Dalit Theology from a Dalit Perspective," in *A Reader in Dalit Theology...*, 141- 142.

[10] Robin Scroggs, as quoted by Christopher Tuckett, *Reading the New Testament: Methods of Interpretation* (London: SPCK, 1987), 141.

[11] Gabriele Dietrich argues, "Dalit theology... has not spent much... energy on the issues of Dalit women... At the same time, Dalit Theologians as well as Dalit movements, have a tendency to be pro-women ideologically". See Dietrich's, *A New Thing on Earth: Hopes and Fears facing Feminist Theology* (Delhi/ Madurai: ISPCK/ TTS, 2001), 242.

[12] Gabriele Dietrich, *A New Thing on Earth: Hopes and Fears facing Feminist Theology*, (Delhi/ Madurai: ISPCK/ TTS, 2001).

forces of gender, class and caste conduct not only as segregated concepts, "but also place specific limitations and produce forms of discrimination in combination."[13] The women were conscientised about their greater discriminatedness, thus amplifying the understanding and the scope of Dalit theology as a liberation theology. For that reason, women's liberation within Dalit theology sought to use Gabriele Dietrich's proposal of challenging internal and domesticating colonies while also dealing with external colonisation.[14] Applying Gabriel's methodological vision of testing and teasing out repressing colonies would give our theologies scope to see the way children in general and girl-children in particular have been bracketed out of our discourses.

Liberative Dialectics of Dalit Consciousness

Dalit consciousness refers to the historical identity of Dalit communities, which is a combination of predominantly awful memories of the longstanding exploitation and subjugation and of the splendid time in the history of sovereignty and autonomy. Memories of pain are also coupled with imminent emancipation, models of which are drawn from various similar histories of suppression. Maria Arul Raja presents the multi-faces of oppression that conditions Dalit consciousness. Dalit consciousness deals with pain of imposed pollution and segregation and the resulting economic impoverishment. It highlights the practical disempowerment created by denial of space for self-governance. He explains how the retention of the

---

[13] Monica Jyotsna Melancthon, "Dalit Readers of the Word: The Quest for Hermeneutics and Method," in *Frontiers in Dalit Hermeneutics*, edited by James Massey and Samson Prabhakar (Bangalore/Delhi: BTESSC-SATHRI/CDSS, 2005), 47

[14] Gabriele Dietrich, "Why should Postcolonial Feminist Theology need to relate to People's Movements?", *Asian Journal of Theology* 19/1 (April 2005): 168

term "Dalit" denotes both "victimhood" and "assertiveness."[15] This paradox has greatly triggered liberative consciousness among Dalits. Jayakumar summarises this notion of Dalit consciousness as:

> A constant reminder of their age-old oppression and their ancient glorious past when their forefathers [sic] were a free people. This has become an expression of hope for them in recovering and enhancing their past identity by expressing their sufferings through drama and poetry.[16]

This has formed the characteristic strength of Dalit theology. As Arvind Nirmal indicates, this consciousness:

> ...reflects the past, the present and the future of Christian Dalits in India. It lays bare the Dalit consciousness and it is this Dalit consciousness which is our primary datum for Christian Dalit theology.[17]

Therefore, "Dalit theology" — as James Massey supposes — should consider "life context, history and language" of the Dalits,[18] which is the "consciousness of their plight as against the natural law, not to speak of ethical or moral laws. This consciousness is new and subject to critique the existing systems, structures and value."[19]

---

[15] Maria Arul Raja, "Perspectives of Dalit Hermeneutics", *Gurukul Journal of Theological Studies* XVI/ 1&2 (Jan. and July, 2005): 23.

[16] Samuel Jayakumar, *Dalit Consciousness and Christian Conversion: Historical Resources for a Contemporary Debate* (Oxford/ Delhi: Regnum International/ ISPCK, 1999), 16.

[17] A. P. Nirmal, "A Dialogue with Dalit Literature", in *Towards A Dalit Theology,* edited by M. E. Prabhakar (Delhi: ISPCK, 1988), 75.

[18] James Massey, *Dalits in India: Religion as a Source of Bondage or Liberation with Special Reference to Christians,* (New Delhi: Manohar Publishers and Distributors, 1995), 173.

[19] James Massey and T. K. John SJ, "Concept Paper: Centre for Dalit/ Subaltern Studies," in *Frontiers in Dalit Hermeneutics,* edited by James Massey, and Samson Prabhakar (Bangalore/ Delhi: BTESSC/ SATHRI & CDSS, 2005), 287.

Emerging challenges like liberalisation, globalisation and other phenomena have baffled Dalit theologians and hermeneuts so much that they are unanimous in their opinion that hermeneutical or methodological tenets of Dalit theology are multi-faceted and have to be open-ended. While the re-look into Dalit Hermeneutics and Praxis[20] is appreciable, it is regrettable that the unique plight of labouring children has not got its particular, in-depth attention of the Dalit think-tank so far. These children get submerged in the huge sea of statistics of the Dalit labour-force and Dalit movement and are, in turn, assimilated into the narratives of the adult world.

Imago Dei and *Body of God* in Dalit Theology

The concept of *Imago Dei* is a fundamental theological point of reference for human beings to work towards its full attainment in their lifestyle and lifetime. It is a notion where the movement of 'image' is from God to human beings and to all creation alike. God stands as the ultimate reference to this image, a coveted status that other beings yearn to achieve. It is a unilateral phenomenon, in the sense that the ultimate adjudication rests with God. Of methodological significance are the questions about who interprets what the image of God is and who bears the image of God. These questions draw into their purview categorisations like theology "from above" and "from below."

---

[20] Of the many Consultations and Seminars held in this direction, a few recent ones could be mentioned here: 1) First International Seminar on "Hermeneutics of Subaltern Praxis with Special Reference to Dalits"-2004, and follow-up Seminar in 2005, organized by CDSS, New Delhi. *Frontiers in Dalit Hermeneutics,* edited by James Massey, and Samson Prabhakar (Bangalore/Delhi: BTESSC-SATHRI/CDSS, 2005) is the outcome of these Seminars. 2) Consultation on "Nurturing Dalit Solidarity", Hyderabad -2007 3) Symposium on "Dalit Theology in the 21st Century: Discordant Voices, Discerning Pathways..."- Kolkata- Jan. 13- 18, 2008.

Deconstructing the picturing of Gods from the dominant Christian and Hindu interpretation, the Dalits would not accept "a non-dalit deity...[to] be the god of dalits."[21] The Dalit image of God is the one:

> ...perceived in Jesus, as not almighty, sovereign Lord but as one who comes in weakness and humility and stands with those despised and suffering people. God is not seen as a ruthless judge demanding a pound of flesh from the sinner but as one who is participating in the agony along with the agonizing people. The power of God is to be interpreted in the serenity of God, i.e. the capacity to share and bear the grief of suffering humanity.[22]

In Dalit theology, drawing on the physical batteredness of the Dalits extends the discourse of the "Image of God" to the "Body of God." This too is resistive in nature in that it demythologises the essential caste hierarchy as emanating from the Body of God as found in classical Hindu tradition. As Dalits did not emanate from the Body of Brahman and are, therefore, outside the caste hierarchy, the Dalit construal of the image of God methodologically interfaces theology and anthropology to make the Dalit-claims for their identity as people of God here and now.

Appraising Colonies within Dalit Theology

In this section, postcolonial criticism—while sympathising with the liberative notion of Dalit theology—sees how in many context-specific issues Dalit theology has inherited dichotomies of sorts that have overlooked the plight of the labouring children from its own community. Such inheritance has created unsolicited colonies.

---

[21] Arvind P. Nirmal, "A Dialogue with Dalit Literature," in *Towards a Dalit Theology*, ed. M. E. Prabhakar (Delhi: ISPCK, 1988), 80.

[22] V. Devasahayam, "The Nature of Dalit Theology as Counter Ideology," in *Frontiers of Dalit Theology...*, 54.

The two important discursive methods of postcolonial criticism that would assist our discussion are "contrapuntality" and "hybridity." *Contrapuntality* is a term that Edward Said proposed to create alternate discourses. This strategy enables "the experiences of the exploited and exploiter to be studied together. To read contrapuntally means to be aware simultaneously of mainstream scholarship and of other scholarship which the dominant discourse tries to domesticate and speaks and acts against."[23] In other words, contrapuntality "retrieves the unheard of voices from the cultural archives."[24] Here, while child labourers have been a part of the oppressed communities, the cultural dominance of adults over children has subdued the voices of the labourers. Contrapuntality helps us recover these voices.

According to Homi Bhabha, "hybridity is an 'in-between space' in which the colonialized translate or undo the binaries imposed by the colonial project." Sugirtharajah adds that hybridity involves a two-way interaction of both colonisers and the colonised towards creating something new.[25] In our study, while the labouring children have contributed to the economy and to the sustenance of community life along side adults, the influence of the activities of children on adult communities has been belittled. Hybridity highlights how enriching community discourses would be if the accomplishment of the children were considered as of definitional significance. This multiplicity of outlook places

---

[23] R. S. Sugirtharajah, *Postcolonial Reconfigurations. An Alternative Way of Reading the Bible and Doing Theology* (London: SCM Press, 2003), 170.

[24] Himanee Gupta, "Reading 'Hinduism' in *Moulin Rouge*," *http://www.psr.edu/pana.cfm?m=159*, (3. 1. 2008).

[25] See R. S. Sugirtharajah, *Postcolonial Criticism and Biblical Interpretation* (Oxford: Oxford University Press, 2002), 22, 191; Bill Ashcroft, Gareth Griffiths and Helen Tiffin, *Key Concepts in Post-Colonial Studies* (London and New York: Routledge, 2004), 118, 139-141; Homi K. Bhabha, *The Location of Culture* (London: Routledge, 1994), 86.

impetus on simultaneous dimensions of a discursive environment. Spaces and time-periods are cut and rearranged in a chronological manner to fit in unknown episodes. It is used to highlight a methodology for knowledge production, and is a useful tool for interrogating the absence of children.

The above-mentioned methodological framework facilitates in unmasking the totalising tendencies of child labour and interrogates the caste-class-gender merger and related dynamics such as power politics, gender politics and identity politics as primary manufacturers of meanings of child labourers. This tool also critically appraises Dalit theology as liberative in nature, but disallows it as having attained an inclusive emancipatory stance for its labouring children. In this light, it tries to examine how Dalit child labourers are hermeneutically overlooked and made "internal exiles" in Dalit theological discourses. A re-look would show how child labourers could be an equally important theological category within the broader framework of Dalit theology. If a theology is the reflection of the Body of God, this evaluation appraises the concept of the Body of God in Dalit theologies.

Dalit theology methodologically esteems liberation as the highest objective to seek and promote. Secondly, it exhibits no pretensions in being biased, subjective and local with the aim to "resist and liberate" and "to disrupt the dominant Western hermeneutical discourse by provincialising it and by the 'reversal of the gaze.'"[26] However, it has also exhibited the traits of inheriting the concerns sometimes unquestioningly.

---

[26] R. S. Sugirtharajah, "Postcolonial Biblical Interpretation," in R. S. Sugirtharajah ed., *Voices from the Margin: Interpreting the Bible from the Third World,* Revised and Expanded Third Edition, (Maryknoll, New York: Orbis Books, 2006), 77.

They could be explained as follows:

1. Dalit theology follows a conventional hierarchal system like patriarchy and adult- children dichotomy. As observed earlier, Dalit feminist hermeneutics exhibited the postcolonial instance of exposing the dominant male representation. With the emergence of feminist hermeneutics, it is more glaring that Dalit adults have represented as authentic the subjugated situation of all the members of Dalit communities, leading to the "hermeneutical forgetness" of the concerns of children, especially the labouring children. Sugirtharajah warns of such colonising in an "eagerness to produce a resistance theory."[27]

2. In the context of this research, either Dalit theology has thought that the labour-market dynamics exploit all its labour force in the same manner or—by its inherent bias—has not addressed the unique forms of exploitation that children undergo in labour market. The labouring children's simultaneous vulnerability in their communities, in their work environment and in the conceptual discourses and theologies provide instances of trans-theological presentation of power discourses. Dalit theology can highlight their insignificant status in the communities, their silenced voices at their labouring locations and their absence in conceptual discourses.

3. While Dalit theology, in principle, does not disclaim the plight of the labouring children, their presence is not treated as significant. It is silent about the meanings that are created and circulated about the labouring children, about the reasons for the creation of such meanings and about the types of identities that are floated, making their oppressed state a non-discourse. Dalit theology can renegotiate and decipher such narratives.

Placing Child Labourers as Theological Category

Dalit theology should define "pain-pathos" as communitarian in nature, in that, it is a combination of the pain and anguish of all

---

[27] R. S. Sugirtharajah, *Postcolonial Reconfigurations...*, 32

the members of the community without qualitatively or quantitatively prioritising adult experience. In its conventional sense, Dalit theology obscures the unique, unrepresented miseries of the children. Child labourers as a theological category would draw into the purview of the methodology not only the plight of the children, but also similar experiences shared by such unrepresented groups. Therefore, like the child labourers, the vulnerability discourse of any group seeks representation in theological discourse.

The profundity of the case of child labourers depends on reflections on their daily life as central to theology and respect for the voices of the marginalised as a guiding norm. It becomes all the more pressing in the case of child labourers that both the adult and economically and culturally dominant voices have eclipsed the labourers' voicelessness or their "still small voice." The paradox, therefore, is that the theology of child labourers has to be initiated not by the child labourers themselves, but by adults, who are, theoretically, dominant. It is the quicker access to resources and the ability to infer that should persuade adults towards this cause. However, the experiences of the children are of primary importance and, therefore, their agential significance[28]

---

[28] Amartya Sen attaches a great deal of importance to "Agency" in his Welfare Economics. He explains that "Agency" takes a wider view of the person, including the various things she/he would want to see happen, and the ability to form such objectives and to have them realised. See his, *On Ethics and Economics...*

John Wall explains how children act as "agency" in disciplines such as sociology, anthropology, history, law and other studies of childhood: "The study of children as agency is the study of how children participate in creating their social environments, exercise their own social competencies, act diversely rather than stereotypically, construct independent ideas and meaning, and help to interpret their own cultures, communities, and identities. Agency also includes 'voice', which 'puts the focus on children's commitment to make known their own ability to act on their own behalf, whether to ensure their own

enlarges the theological canvas as well as sharpens the lens. Reflection on children embodies the theological conviction that the divine manifests in the mundane and that genuine liberation must occur in the most commonplace of places—in the embodied lives of children.[29]

A Critical Review of Some Hermeneutics of Childhood Studies

To formulate some hermeneutical tools to theologically understand child labour, some clues could be drawn from the hermeneutics of childhood studies, in general, that are, however, of increasing interest in the western academia. Their presence, nevertheless, would shed some light on our discussion in our particular context. Hermeneutical keys advocated in these thoughts add to those culled out through employing postcolonial criticism. Regarding the childhood hermeneutical discourses in the west, John Wall summarises the approaches under the following models: [30]

The Communitarian Approach

Stanley Hauerwas, Jean Bethke Elshtain and Gilbert Meilander popularised this approach in the 1980s. They draw on thinkers like Aristotle, Augustine, Thomas Aquinas and John Calvin. This model takes a "top-down" approach of the modernity philosophy where the upbringing of the children is to be modeled on

---

interests or to modify the world that surrounds them.'" What many social sciences "reveal is not just children's distinctive capabilities and agency—important though these are—but rather, in a more complex way, the kinds of *tension* that exist between children's agency and their larger surrounding worlds. John Wall, "Childhood Studies, Hermeneutics, and Theological Ethics"..., 538, 543.

[29] Bonnie J. Miller-McLemore, "Children and Religion in the Public Square: Too Dangerous and Too Safe, Too Difficult and Too Silly," *JR* 86/ 3 (July 2006), 401.

[30] John Wall, "Childhood Studies, Hermeneutics, and Theological Ethics," *JR* 86/ 4 (Oct. 2006), 529- 537.

traditionally established norms and values. Here, adults, especially parents, are the models to look up to. The community or the family would be the agency or the voice of the children.

The Liberationist Approach

Ethicists and hermeneuts such as Kathleen and James McGinnis, Cornel West, Herbert Anderson, Pamela Couture and Adrian Thatcher, while critically adopting their insights from the communitarian model, assume a "bottom-up" approach where children's own lives, unheard voices, unconsulted agency and undeserving experiences are the primary markers towards understanding childhood concerns and the reign of God. They are patterned on liberationist movements and take grass roots experiences earnestly.

The Progressive Familism

This approach gets it name from its affinity to liberationism and feminism ("progressive") and indicates that the welfare of the children relies on adults' conviction about the children, especially the conviction of the families ("familism"). This considers children both as *they are* ("given") and what they *would be* ("developmental"). This would mould them as "competent social agents." In the mid 1990s, scholars like Don Browning, Lisa Sowle Cahill, Bonnie Miller-McLemore and others presented this model. They offer an interdisciplinary approach in dealing with these issues and, therefore, develop refined hermeneutical perspectives.

Postmodern Hermeneutical Circle

In a context where historical accounts and their interpretations belong to adult domain, the "postmodern hermeneutical circle" as explicated by John Wall includes both children and adults as sources of meaning, although the degree of participation varies because the circle constitutes adult perspectives so far. Positively, the children are insiders to the meaning-making exercises. Secondly, being insiders would aid children's cause because it opens up a plethora of breakthroughs in studying children as at once associates in the common social world. However, this demands highly responsible and responsive adults. Wall goes on to explaining that children's "otherness" can be recognised without "othering' them. A question continues to remain crucial: "Who controls the hermeneutical circle?" Wall suggests:

> The underlying problem is not how to make children equal research participants. It is how to interpret the meaning and status of children in their 'otherness', when children more than any other group cannot fully interpret their own otherness for themselves.[31]

Need for an Applicable Hermeneutical Approach

The above models have highlighted a dedicated view of the child to be in the centre of our discourses, while their culturally constructed vulnerabilities and limitations could be addressed at various levels. Extending these views to the vulnerabilities of the child labourers, the above hermeneutical discussions could be more accommodative in the following areas:

- They underestimate the impact on children's lives of the larger economical, political and global conditions so that children may need more than just an initiation into the world of attributed meanings and constructed identities.

- In the above models, the focus on children is from the perspective of family or community, i.e., familial interaction as emancipatory means/paradigm. Therefore, they become subset of family studies. However, such studies do not address the debates on the lives of labourers who are directly related to many social structures and agencies. Children's identity is drawn in the conventional pattern where complete

---

[31] John Wall, "Childhood Studies, Hermeneutics, and Theological Ethics,"…, 537.

subservience is thought of as a way of functioning especially through marriage and parenting.

- Children as contributors (unfortunately through sacrificing their childhood and identity through harsh labouring) to the economy are left out completely. The above models lead us to an unpleasant paradox in our situation. While the presence of children in the family conceptually denotes the presence of God, even the financial contribution is in a way material blessing to their families. If, in this sense, children are God's economy of liberation from starvation, are we promoting a benign form of "God's presence"? The postmodern approach reinstates oppressive strands along with liberative opportunities. While the child labourers' voices and concerns come to the fore, adults continue to be "custodians" of values and culture at least for a considerable period of time.

Child Labourers as a Theological Category: Methodological Issues

Theological Discourses on Child Labour with a Methodological Framework

While formulating a theology of child labour, one could be drawn into the intricacies of a multi-foci debate that could impinge on the freedom of innocent children and on the understanding of extending the values of God's reign. Therefore, it involves a thorough critique of our vantage points in the largely adult-centered theories and biblical interpretation that have either damaged or sidelined the harsh realities of child labour. It also evaluates the contributing factors of child labour and the instruments that implement and govern the constitutional remedies. This takes us adults—more so for the victims themselves—to the enormous task of culling God and Good News in hopelessness and despair.

Theological Discourses on Child Labour as Inter-generational

If the labouring children were the subjects of theologising, and such theologising were to be aimed for their liberation, then the methodological questions are: Who could represent their plight better than the children themselves? In the case of child labourers, it is precisely the fact that they could not voice out their grievances and organise themselves for resistance is taken advantage of by those who exploit children and childhood. In a situation like this, how far can genuinely committed adults, who are the supposedly possible representatives, take up the cause of labouring children and understand their plight fully? How far are they able to overcome the inter- generational divide? As one notices, it is the adults who mostly voice out the concerns of the labouring children. Some of these representatives would themselves have trod this path of exploitation in their childhood and would have emerged to represent these children with genuine experience. Some others—as parents who have given care to the children—claim to represent the cause of children equally genuinely.[32] Some go further to mention how "childhood studies should not only apply existing theological methods and norms but challenge and

---

[32] Feminist Maternal Theologians are some of the voices that attempt to understand children "precisely because they have stood where the children have stood, at the intersection of society's contradictory outward idealization and subtle devaluation of child care and children." The feminist maternal theology offers four persuasive directions. "First, the demand to give privileged voice to the marginalized is extended to mothers and children. Second, [it] challenges the contradictory demonization and idealization of children and women's bodies in the acts of bearing and raising children. Third, it enriches debates about theological doctrines of Christian love, sin, and grace by turning to the child. Finally, [it] stretches claims for justice and liberation across differences to include children and mothers for whom the democratic principle of equality based on formal identity or sameness with the adult male simply does not work." Bonnie J. Miller-McLemore, "Children and Religion in the Public Square: Too Dangerous and Too Safe, Too Difficult and Too Silly," *JR* 86/ 3 (July 2006), 398- 400.

transform them."[33] Methodologically, a journey back to our childhood memories and experiences could help us to evaluate the privileged and deprived positions.

Theological Discourses on Child Labour to Be both Conceptual and Praxiological

For the children wronged-against, this lifestyle—unless informed—would be existentially "given." The "thrill" of making a living in their childhood would have been at the core of their existential reality unless and until they are introduced and conscientised to a whole world and time of childhood, educational purposes, welfare and the consequent opportunities in life as fulfillment of their dreams.[34] This requires a participatory method where researchers and representatives would comprehend what the children desire and retrieve the painful experiences that have gone unrepresented. This involves dedicated bias in interacting with religious traditions (predominantly oral), the way the child labourers would re-look at the cultural, religious beliefs and practices they are constantly in interaction with and their aspirations to reach higher professional positions that would shock many. Through the interpretation of their pathos, through material contribution and through their interaction and wisdom, they are capable of springing up new accounts of their selves that reverberate past occasions as exemplified in some of the sources of theologising.

---

[33] John Wall calls this approach "Childism." In Wall's words, "the question for theological ethics is how to respond to the complex lives of children in the contemporary world in a sufficiently attentive and meaningful a way as to enrich, in turn, theological ethical understanding itself." John Wall, "Childhood Studies, Hermeneutics, and Theological Ethics," *JR* 86/4 (Oct. 2006), 523-524.

[34] This is my observation in my interaction with child labourers during the last four years.

Some of the present scientific tools operate within rigorous categories with quantifiable representations and oversimplification. The indeterminate social reality is beyond one's research ability to box-up. Such seamless discursive space helps in uncovering concealed stories/narratives of the child labourers from within the dominant narratives against which and as part of which the children act. It assists in recovering the "Emancipatory Potential of Knowledge" as well.[35]

Theology as a Monitoring Agency

Approaching the issue of child labourers theologically calls our theologies to be all eyes and discernment for a more comprehensible and unambiguous analysis of our social structures. It also calls for non-pretensions that adults cannot think and theologise from the point of view of child labourers. One wonders how many can empathise with the inherent trauma that the child labourers have undergone. However, this is to our best extent worth an endeavor—by revisiting our own childhood times. As Capps mentions, "For adults, listening to the previously submerged voice of the child inside is a painful experience. It can also, however, be a liberating experience."[36]

Hermeneutical Considerations of Child Labourers as a Theological Category

A theological discourse on child labour is of *Kairotic* significance. An attempt to formulate hermeneutical keys towards a theology

---

[35] Felix Wilfred, "Towards Liberative Social Sciences: Dialogue with Liberation Theology," in *Creative Social Research: Rethinking Theories and Methods,* edited by Ananta Kumar Giri (New Delhi: Vistaar Publications, 2004), 75

[36] Donald Capps, "Religion and Child Abuse: Perfect Together" *JSSR,* 31/1(March 1992), 1- 14.

http://links.jstor.org/sici?sici=00218294per cent28199203per cent2931per centper cent3A1per cent3C1per cent3ARACAPTper cent3E2.0.COper cent3B2-P (22. 1. 2008).

of child labour is through an interactive and affirmative way of perceiving and restructuring some of the theological formulations pointing towards the tangible ends. These postures can be arrived at through looking into some of the hermeneutical necessities proposed below:

(1) *Children as possessing the Image of God and therefore Co-creators with God*

Children at every stage of their life exhibit the image of God. Through this bearing they are creators of the meaning/s of theological significance and re-interpreters of phrases like "image of God", "God's Image", "creation", etc. The concept of "Image of God" as manifested in every being emancipates the oppressed from the imposed notion of thinking of themselves as fateful and gives them a new self-esteem as persons. The scope of the "Image of God" is restricted to the essence of a person alone; it also includes human bodies. Jesus as a human child not only shared in the essence of God, but also took the physical body towards a total manifestation of the constant recreation of the Image. In extension, this eminence generates in children the energy to be in constant interaction with self, with God and with community to ever re-create the image, and thus constantly participate in the enterprise of re-creation towards greater life. Both children and God would gladly wish to wear an image thus created.

Of critical importance is the discussion between theological category "Image of God" and the cultural construct of the "Image of a child" (childhood). While the image-of-child discourse leads us to what we can do for children in their vulnerability and what they can do in their best spirit, the Image-of-God discourse helps us place them on par with (perhaps, at times, above) adults. Towner has this to say about the systemic neglect of "child" in the "image of God" discourse:

> Although biblical scholars have explored and examined the term in depth and offered rich interpretations of it, they have

rarely directly discussed the term in relationship to children. Theologians and ethicists who build on the work of biblical scholars and the notion of the image of God to articulate contemporary perspectives on human rights or human dignity have also generally neglected to include children.[37]

Is this manner of restoration of the image of God in the child labourers an attempt to restore the identity and dignity of children for God's sake or to restore the identity and dignity of child labourers themselves? Do we not, by reinstating the dignity of the child labourers, reinstate God's identity? In other words, are we not taking up a "task of making God exist"?[38] A declaration in the same vein can be, "God exists in good shape if child labourers exist in good shape." This concept has revolutionary potential. This calls for the re-focusing of the discussion on children as a public-private task that aims to "cultivate children's fully human social creativity as images of their Creator." [39]

(2) *Child Labourers as Full-Citizens*

Here, the conceptual "Image of God" encompassing the physical self takes a practical political stance leading to their full rights. Child labourers, in particular, and children, in general, should be treated as full citizens of the State. The issues of the physically battered bodies of the children and their stunted growth become central to the hermeneutical task. Citizens should be protected not only from defamed definitions and meanings, but also from

---

[37] Sibley Towner W, "Children and the Image of God" in, Marcia Bunge ed. *The Child in the Bible* (Michigan/ Cambridge: W. B. Eerdmans Publishing Company), 308.

[38] This is the title of an article by Joan Casanas, a Roman Catholic Priest from Spain

[39] John Wall, "Fatherhood, Childism, and the Creation of Society," *http://muse.jhu.edu/journals/journal of the american academy of religion/toc/ aar75.1.html.* (Jan. 15, 2008).

the physicality of violence. Children are knowledgeable subjects, exhibiting their own religious and political thoughts. As observed earlier, citizenship is endowed on persons who are entitled the rights and expected to fulfill responsibilities. While citizenship, to a great extent, means a functional relationship between the citizens and the State, the State's obligation towards grooming children should get greater policy attention. Until then, state policies project a patchy institution of citizenship. This calls for a more responsible adult world that possesses resources and power to float discourses and meanings. This is preferential and not charitable.

The hermeneutical task here is to take children's own insights seriously because they are fully humans and continue to exhibit it at different stages of their lives. This is an attempt to observe the images of the crushed innocent beings alongside God's image. Therefore, the process of restoration poses crucial theological questions. Digression from such objectives is repugnance for the values of God's reign. This calls for a constant interaction between Human Rights and Child Rights, where both creatively negotiate to overcome their biases against children towards seeing full humans in children.

(3) *Child Labour's Experience of Exploitation as Unique*

Perhaps the explicit absence of children and child labourers from liberative discourses is due to the perception that adult experience enshrines all understanding and knowledge and, therefore, an absolute point of reference. Such conceptions subsume the unique harrowing conditions that children undergo. As discussed earlier, the labour market profits on children's non-resilient nature, where childhood is commodified as subservient identities for lesser wages, for dismal physical welfare, for deprivement of childhood necessities and for an insecure future. Their inability for an organised rebellion is converted into a profit-making sector. More specifically in the context of labouring girl-children, girls face greater sexual abuse. The victims fear to share such ordeal either due to the social stigma attached to such experiences, or their own inability to comprehend the intriguing dynamics of the existence or seriousness of such abuse.

In all these spheres, adults are better off and, therefore, cannot represent the child labourers' plight comprehensively. While this does not take away from adults the obligation to voice out the plight of children, such responsibilities should not turn into a patronising act as know-all and end-all.

(4) *Engaged Epistemology: Adult-Child Interdependence*

While the available discourses are from the adult domain, this hermeneutical direction emphasises the significance of childhood in formulating adulthood. Attention is given to the way children have been separated from adult self-reflection. The study attempts to show how living with children most fundamentally takes the form of a dialogue, in which the ontological horizons of the adult and the child become linked in an unending tête-à-tête.

The positivistic and essentialist worldview makes children objects, appropriate only for controlled analysis and social operation, perhaps, but removed from the indispensable correlation with the wider adult community. The idea of "participation" as a model for religious education not only means children's "initiation" into a religious tradition, but also taking children's own insights seriously, coming from a stage in itself. John Wall suggests the need for:

> ...both the social self-creativity of the adults around [the children] and the gradual development of social self- creative capabilities within children themselves. These have their beginnings in children's play and imagination, but they also need to be nurtured into competencies for engaging with and changing society. All of us to one degree or another desire not only to participate in society for ourselves, but also to

have society respond in turn to our own incapabilities, vulnerabilities, and dependencies.[40]

The "incapabilities, vulnerabilities, and dependence" could possibly redefine the term "children of God" and the insecurities could be converted into positive energies through inter-generational reliability. This, methodologically, takes adults back to their childhood imaginations and aspirations and to the times when they needed greater sustenance from their seniors. This approach is not in the model of patronising but as responsibilities towards one another. This foresees the much-aspired "Inclusive-Communities."

(5) *Aspirations and Dreams of Child Labourers as Commencement for Concrete Solutions*

While the *experience* of deprived childhood of these labourers is crucial, their crushed innocence, throttling environment and deprived identity as sources of liberative narratives enrich the discourse. Another point is the aspirations that these children express and interpret. These aspirations, as I have pointed out earlier, are often judged as larger-than-required dreams of the labouring children, because such aspirations would challenge the popular rational ingenuity outside the hermeneutical circle of crushed innocence. From the point of view of the labourers, the activity of aspiration is both interrogatory and creative. The aspirations interrogate the systemic fallacy that deprived them of their aspired position, while they are creative in inducing the momentum of liberation towards the desired dream. As Sen observes, dreams and desires are courageous reflections in "unfavourable circumstances."[41]

---

[40] John Wall, "Childhood Studies, Hermeneutics, and Theological Ethics" ..., 546.

[41] Amartya Sen, *On Ethics and Economics...*, 60.

Child labourers construct their dreams for their future on the fulfilled desires of the privileged children they interact with. For instance, many child labourers wish to be doctors or teachers or engineers when they grow up, with their innocent minds not aware of the fact that the education they have had/not had would not take them to those professions.[42] Such desires are common among children of that age whether or not they are groomed towards them. Even those groomed towards that may not reach the desired end. Therefore, providing each child the due opening and opportunity towards the preferred end is the fundamental task of such theologising. This provides theology a location to have children as the subjects of theology by allowing them to dream and to fulfill cravings as one among the many significant points of theologising. The social self-creative capabilities within children are to be explored. These capabilities find roots in children's recreation and imagination, but they also need to be nurtured into their potentialities for connecting with and influencing society. As Clarke rationalises, the "theology of aspiration, self-narration and alternate discourse" is an indicator of subaltern discourses that initiate "creative and self-actualizing space, which generates… self-reflectivity quite regardless of the governing discourse of the dominant…"[43]

---

[42] Godwin Shiri and Rohan Gideon, "*The Plight of Female Child Labourers,*"…, 57.

[43] Sathianathan Clarke, "Dalit Theology: An Introductory and Interpretive Theological Exposition," A Paper presented at Kolkota Symposium entitled *Dalit Theology in the 21st Century: Discordant Voices, Discerning Pathways,* January 13, 2008, 13.

CHAPTER 4

Challenges of Child Labour for Christian Ministry in India

When the members of our community fail to live up to our responsibilities to prevent abuse and to help survivors of abuse heal and find justice, our community is more than just irresponsible: we are guilty of enabling and perpetuating abuse.[1]

This study attempts to move beyond the "adults-only" frame of mind and shows how living with child labourers basically takes the form of a dialogue, in which the growing spheres of adults and children are collaborated in an eternal theological conversation. The dynamics include the unrelenting influence of children in the adult experience of God and the values of God's reign in society. Children should be seen as "persons" and full members of religious communities. Children are competent subjects, with their own religious ideas. Traditionally, theology has described children, especially the labouring children as those with low human aptitude particularly to comprehend God and to interact within members of the community. The hermeneutical task of interpreting the labouring circumstances of the children

---

[1] Rabbi Mark Dratch: "A Community of Co- enablers" in Amy Neustein ed, *Tempest in the Temple: Jewish Communities and Child Sex Scandals*, (Lebanon: Brandeis University Press, 2009), 105.

in the light of the Scriptures and liberative narratives is imperative. This brings to the purview of liberative interpretative schemes the ontologically designed deprivations that have found safe homes in dominant theologies and ideologies, even those with the liberative outlook.

Douglas Strum builds up a compelling rationale for the freedom of children and childhood. The adult-child discourse is supposedly the "last strongholds of domination, parallel to master-slave and male-female relationships of the past, and hence constitutes a final frontier for liberation theology."[2] This research has attempted to formulate and present some hermeneutical leads that seek to theologically evaluate and understand the unfortunate state of child labourers towards their liberation. The NCEUS report is optimistic of the complete elimination of child labour by 2014. While this work has not given up such optimism, the elimination of child labour still seems to be a far cry until certain rehabilitation processes are initiated to educate children and to create employment opportunities to the families that would lose the income of the working children thus schooled.

The issues of child labour in India, in particular, and the issues of child rights, in general, stare both pathetically and challengingly at our theological rigidities. Considering the slow and discouraging initiative by theological fraternity as well as the state, this work has attempted to retrieve similar traditions in the Bible that have devaluated and exploited children. But this sense of loss for children is laid back by powerful traditions of the significance of childhood that Christianity has inherited. The epistemological significance thus recovered helps in reinterpreting Soteriology, Christology and Ecclesiology from the point of view of children,

---

[2] Cited by Bonnie J. Miller- McLemore, "Children and Religion in the Public Square,"…, 394.

childhood and child labourers.[3] Therefore, we can perceive children as the full images of God and full humans who claim full attention in the Church. In the State, child labourers as full citizens are obliged to receive greater attention and privileges. While this claim sees them on par with adults on many fronts, child labourers' experiences of exploitation are unique and not to be homogenised with adult experiences of exploitation. Their vulnerability due to their physical and mental condition should allow the methodology of engaged epistemology where adults and children are interdependent for knowledge formulation. In such positions, the aspirations and dreams of child labourers provide points of commencement for concrete actions for their emancipation from stereotyped notions. The discriminatory notions have been uncritically perpetuated by sacraments like baptism and Eucharist and by ecclesiological practices like Sunday school and other children education programmes, because our worships and activities are not child-friendly.

Therefore, if theology is redemptive in nature, how often has the package of theological education been put to a critical scrutiny, especially with the issues of "labour-relations"? Largely, our theologies do not represent labour woes completely and, therefore, theological discourses reinforce the *status quo* — and so a paradox between theologising and labour.

The aforementioned proposals that challenge our ministry present possibilities for evolving multi-dimensional resistance to the popular negligence of children's concerns. This necessitates a movement that is hermeneutically conversational and practically collaborational: conversation between child rights conventions and positive picturisation of children in scriptures and collaboration of the ministry of the Church among children with child rights

---

[3] A recent work on Christology and children at risk in India is by Jesudason B. Jeyaraj, *"Child in the Midst: Incarnation and Child Theology"* in Children at Risk: Issues and Challenges (Delhi: ISPCK: 2009).

movements. The proposed hermeneutical leads re-examine the situatedness of child labourers in the theological discourses so far in dialogue with the existing adult-centred discourses. When the place of children and their aspirations are recognised as those that matter religiously, culturally and socially, the values of God's reign are tangibly translated. This, however, requires many "border-crossings", perhaps many of them unheard of. This is imperative, especially when there is a purposeful violation of dialogical circumstances between emancipation and rehabilitation. Fundamental to such exercises should be the identity of child labourers. This provides a point of reference from which the historically and socially created boundaries could be critiqued and negotiated.

Here, one should recognise the emergence of movements to address children issues. Child Theology Movement, Global Alliance for Holistic Child Development and similar forums have laid new foundations for innovative ways of doing theology with children at the centre. Now the theological universities in our part of the world have woken up to the needs of the children with a hesitant charitable space at the moment to initiate introductory discourses. Much more needs to be done to make children's perspective a major for theological praxis. If these perspectives are nipped in the bud or snubbed as insignificant and immature, our theological methods would be impoverished of what Martin Marty calls in his book *The Mystery of the Child* "the child's openness to wonder as we grow old." Emphasising this mystery, Marty calls us to be "drawn into seeing the world in their angle" and to be "more open to the mystery, more responsive to others, more receptive."

The method emphasised here is a dialogical approach, in which the resources of adults and children are placed for an on-going discourse. The dynamics include the unrelenting influence of children's experience of oppression and vulnerability on adult experience in the Church and society calling for intergenerational discourses. If theology is a reflection of the life lived here and now, this dialogical process should seep down to every context. This is where children's views—through their own ways—can be participatory in a multi-experiential context.

On the other hand, theologies—as perceived—project their objectives based on their understanding of God and the value they attach to God's creatures. It is this notion "that must, therefore, be respected in the relations human beings establish with one another and with other kind of beings in the world."[4] This provides a vantage point from which the inter-generational theological interaction and dialogue could be initiated. This dialogue is imperative because the Creator "labours patiently to bring creation to perfection" and "the creator is ... as one who is in dialogue with creation at its different stages."[5] It is this dialogical labour that reshapes even our understanding of God, the image of God and, therefore, the Body of God. This model would guide Dalit theology to incorporate the dialogical nature of theologising, which would simultaneously enrich its interpretive activity and, in turn, offer models for incorporating the pathos of the labouring children.

While this research is largely confined to the experiences of the child labourers coming from marginalised castes and tribes and approached through an appraisal of the recent theological thinking in India, other frameworks for discussions on child labour can be drawn into the liberative spirit of theological praxis. They could analyse child-related issues from inter-religious perspectives, specific focus on girl-child labourers from a gender perspective, theological-anthropological evaluation of the dignity

---

[4] Kathryn Tanner, "Theology and Anthropology," *ThT* L/ 4 (Jan. 1994): 567.

[5] Rosemary Nixon, "Images of the Creator in Gen. 1 and 2," *ThT* XCVII/ 777 (May- June, 1994): 188, 192.

of children in the light of child rights/human rights, their place in the Body of God, etc. This research has tried to interrogate some of these ground realities directing a few discussions; more needs to be "done" than "said" in this regard.

History has proved that issues of rights have made an impact through movements like Dalit liberation movements, women's empowerment movements, eco-concerns movements and so on. Child rights movements are strongly established and spreading all over the world. However, they are still knocking on the doors of our theologies. As in the above case, theologies have been enriched by movements, and now movements can be treated as powerful theological texts. George Zachariah mentions that it is imperative and possible as our "embededness" in our context commits us to "engage in public witnessing in communion with the social movements... to bring about radical social transformation."[6] This interdependability enriches our "doing" style of theology effectively. Our own experiences of childhood challenges, which are deeply embedded in us and have moulded our upbringing, can give thoughts to our "doing" theology with children at risk.

This research potentially opens up further to studies in interfacing the recently emerged child theology and child rights movement in Christian education. This would mean making children aware of their place and rights and their worth in God's sight. The richness of such theological considerations as the economy of God's liberative acts can enhance community spirituality by exhibiting the day-to-day activities that are sometimes denounced.

---

[6] George Zachariah, "Christian Theologizing and Social Thinking in India: Political Perspectives" in his paper read at the National Network for Young Theologians in India, (ECC: Bangalore, April 23-25, 2010).

Bibliography

BOOKS

Ana, Julio de Santa, ed. *Separation Without Hope: Essays on the Relation between the Church and the Poor during the Industrial Revolution and the Western Colonial Expansion*. Geneva: World Council of Churches, 1978.

Ashcroft, Bill, Gareth Griffiths and Helen Tiffin. *Key Concepts in Post-Colonial Studies*. London and New York: Routledge, 2004.

Balch, David L. and Carolyn Osiek ed. *Early Christian Families in Context: An Interdisciplinary Dialogue*. Grand Rapids: William B. Eerdmans Publishing Company, 2003.

Barth, Karl. *Church Dogmatics* III/4. Translated by G. W. Bromiley and R. J. Ehrlich. Edinburgh: T & T Clarke, 1960.

Bhabha, Homi K. *The Location of Culture*. London: Routledge, 1994.

Bieler, Andre. "Gradual Awareness of Social, Economic Problem (1750-1900)." In *Separation Without Hope? Essays on the Relation between the Church and the Poor During the Industrial Revolution and the Western Colonial Expansion*. Edited by Julio de Santa Ana. Geneva: World Council of Churches, 1978.

Blomfield Jackson, Trans. *The Treatise De Spiritu Sancto: The Nine Homilies of the Hexaemeron and the Letters of St. Basil the Great Archbishop of Caesarea*. Vol 8 of *NPNF*, 2nd Series. Grand Rapids, Michigan: Wm. B. Eerdmans Publishing Company, 1955.

Bunge, Marcia J, ed. *The Child in Christian Thought*. Grand Rapids, Michigan: William B. Eerdmans Publishing Company, 2001.

Centre of Social Research. *Working Condition of Children Employed in Unorganised Sector-A Case in Sivakasi.* Madras: 1984.

Clarke, Sathianathan. *Dalits and Christianity: Subaltern Religion and Liberation Theology in India.* Delhi: Oxford University Press, 1998.

__________. "Exploration of Intercultural Theological Methodologies in Asia: Curing Culture Lethargy and Culling Theological Directionalities." In *Intercultural Asian Theological Methodologies: An Exploration.* Edited by Samson Prabhakar. Bangalore: SATHRI, 2002.

Crossan, John Dominic. *The Historical Jesus: The Life of a Mediterranean Jewish Peasant.* San Francisco: Harper, 1991.

Devasahayam V. *Frontiers of Dalit Theology,* ed. Madras: ISPCK/ GURUKUL, 1997.

Dietrich, Gabriele. *A New Thing on Earth: Hopes and Fears Facing Feminist Theology.* Delhi/ Madurai: ISPCK/ TTS, 2001.

Dirks, Nicolas B "The Invention of Caste: Civil Society in Colonial India." In *Identity, Consciousness and the Past: Forging of Caste and Community in India and Sri Lanka.* Edited by Seneviratne H.L. Delhi: Oxford University Press, 1999.

Ferguson, Everett. *Backgrounds of Early Christianity.* Second edition. Grand Rapids, Michigan: William B. Eerdmans Publishing Company, 1993.

Finn, Thomas M. *The Early Christian Baptism and the Catechumenate: West and East Syria.* Minnesota: The Liturgical Press, 1992.

Geeta Chowdhry and Sheila Nair, eds. *Power, Postcolonialism and International Relations: Reading Race, Gender and Class.* First Indian reprint. London and New York: Routledge, 2003.

Geiko Muller- Fahrenholz ed. , *and do not hinder them: an ecumenical plea for the admission of children to the eucharist.* Geneva:World Council of Churches, 1982.

Indian Social Institute. *State of Human Rights in India 1998.* New Delhi: ISI, 1999.

Jayakumar, Samuel. *Dalit Consciousness and Christian Conversion: Historical Resources for a Contemporary Debate.* Oxford/ Delhi: Regnum International/ ISPCK, 1999.

Jolly, Richard and Cornia, Andrea Giovanni. The Impact of World Recession on Children. UNICEF, 1984.

Kabeer, Naila, Geetha B. Nambissan and Ramya Subramanian, eds. *Child Labour and the Right to Education in South Asia: Needs Versus Rights.* New Delhi: Sage Publications, 2003.

Khatu, K. K. *The Working Children in India.* Baroda Operation Research Group, 1983.

Kulshreshta, J. C. *Child Labour in India.* New Delhi: Ashish Publishing House, 1978.

Larbeer, Mohan P. *Ambedkar on Religion: A Liberative Perspective.* Madurai/Delhi: DRC/ISPCK, 2003.

Marty, Martin. *The Mystery of the Child.* Michigan/ Cambridge: William B. Eerdmans Publishing Company, 2007

Massey, James. *Dalits in India: Religion as a Source of Bondage or Liberation with Special Reference to Christians.* New Delhi: Manohar, 1995.

Massey James and Samson Prabhakar, eds, *Frontiers in Dalit Hermeneutics.* Bangalore/Delhi: BTESSC-SATHRI/CDSS, 2005.

Meeks, Douglas M. *God the Economist: The Doctrine of God and Political Economy.* Mineapolis: Fortress Press, 1989.

Mohanty, Manoranjan. *Class, Caste and Gender.* New Delhi: Sage, 2004.

Nalunnakkal, George Mathew. *Green Liberation: Towards an Integral Ecotheology.* Delhi: IPSCK/NCCI, 1999.

Nieuwenhuys, Olga. "The Paradox of Child Labour and Anthropology." In *The Oxford India Companion to Sociology and Anthropology* Vol 2. Edited by Veena Das. New Delhi: Oxford University Press, 2003.

Nirmal, Arvind P, ed. *A Reader in Dalit Theology.* Madras: GURUKUL, 1991.

Oommen, George and John C.B. Webster, eds. *Local Dalit Christian History*. Delhi: ISPCK, 2002.

Paul, Pope John II. *Encyclicals*. Trivandrum: Carmel International Publishing House, 2005.

Phan, Peter C. *Social Thought*. Wilmington, Delaware: Michael Glazier Inc., 1984.

Pontifical Council for Justice and Peace. *Work as Key to the Social Question: The Great Social and Economic Transformations and the Subjective Dimension of Work*. Vatican City: Libreria Editrice Vaticana, 2002.

Prabhakar M. E. *Towards a Dalit Theology*, ed. Delhi: ISPCK, 1988.

Rauschenbusch, Walter. *The Social Principles of Jesus*. New York: Association Press, 1927.

Robb, Peter. *Dalit Movement and the Meaning of Labour in India*. Delhi: Oxford University Press, 1993.

Samuel, Simon. *A Postcolonial Reading of Mark's Story of Jesus*. London: T & T Clarke, 2007.

Schaff, Philip. *NPNF* Vol IX. Grand Rapids, Michigan: Wm. B. Eerdmans Publishing Company, 1956.

Schmemann, Alexander. *Of Water and the Spirit*. Crestwood, NY: St. Vladimir's Seminary Press, 1995.

Sen, Amartya. *On Ethics and Economics*. New Delhi: Oxford University Press, 1987.

__________. *Identity and Violence: The Illusion of Destiny*. London: Allen Lane, 2006.

Sharda, Neel K. *The Legal, Economic and Social Status of the Indian Child*. New Delhi: National Book Organisation, 1988.

State of Human Rights in India 1998. New Delhi: Indian Social Institute, 1999.

Stiglitz, Joseph. *Globalization and Its Discontents*. New Delhi: Penguin, 2002

Stuckelberger, Christoph. *Global Trade Ethics: An Illustrated Overview.* Geneva: WCC Publications, 2002.

Sugirtharajah R.S. *Postcolonial Criticism and Biblical Interpretation.* Oxford: Oxford University Press, 2002.

__________. "Bible Studies after the Empire". In *The Postcolonial Bible.* Edited by R. S. Sugirtharajah. Sheffield: Sheffield Academic Press, 1998.

__________. "Postcolonial Biblical Interpretation." In. *Voices from the Margin: Interpreting the Bible from the Third World.* Edited by R. S. Sugirtharajah. Revised and Expanded Third Edition. Maryknoll, New York: Orbis Books, 2006.

__________. *Postcolonial Reconfigurations. An Alternative Way of Reading the Bible and Doing Theology.* London: SCM Press, 2003.

The Constitution of India and Child Labour. Mysore: CACL, 2003.

Thumma, Anthoniraj. *Wisdom of the Weak: Foundation of People's Theology.* Delhi: ISPCK, 2000.

Towner, Sibley W. "Children and the Image of God" in Marcia Bunge Edited *The Child in the Bible* (Michigan/ Cambridge: W. B. Eerdmans Publishing Company), 307- 323.

Tuckett, Christopher. *Reading the New Testament: Methods of Interpretation.* London: SPCK, 1987.

Varghese, Baby. *Baptism and Chrismation in the Syriac Tradition.* Kottayam: SEERI.

Verner, David C. *The Household of God: The Social World of the Pastoral Epistles.* California: Scholars Press, 1983.

Weber, Hans-Ruedi. *Jesus and the Children: Biblical Resources for Study and Preaching.* Geneva: World Council of Churches, 1979.

Webster, John C.B. *Dalit Christians: A History.* New Delhi: ISPCK, 1996.

Wielenga, Bastian. *Labour-Serving God or Mammon?* Delhi: ISPCK, 1987.

__________. *Biblical Perspectives on Labour.* Madurai: Tamil Nadu Theological Seminary, 1982.

Wilfred, Felix. *The Sling of Utopia.* Delhi: ISPCK, 2005.

__________. *On the Banks of Ganges: Doing Contextual Theology*. Delhi: ISPCK, 2002.

__________. "Towards Liberative Social Sciences: Dialogues with Liberation Theology." In *Creative Social Research: Rethinking Theories and Methods*. Edited by Ananta Kumar Giri. New Delhi: Vistaar Publications, 2004.

World Development Report 2000/2001: *Attacking Poverty*. New York: Oxford University Press, 2000.

Wright, Shelley. *International Human Rights, Decolonization and Globalisation: Becoming Human*. London: Routledge, 2001.

JOURNALS

Ahmed, Iftikhar. "Getting Rid of Child Labour." *EPW*, 34/27 (July 3, 1999): 1815-1822.

Anandhi S. "Caste and Gender in Colonial South India." *EPW* 40/15 (2005): 1518-1522

Archana Mehendale. "Children's Rights: Lessons on Monitoring." *EPW* Vol 34/16 (April 17-23, 2004): 1568-1570

Avtar Singh, "Child Labour Problems and Prospects: Socio-Legal Measures." *SA* 54/4 (Oct-Dec): 396-97.

Bonnie J. Miller- McLemore. "Children and Religion in the Public Square: Too Dangerous and Too Safe, Too Difficult and Too Silly." *JR* 86/ 3 (July 2006): 398- 400.

Bunge, Marcia J. "The Child, Religion and the Academy: Developing Robust Theological and Religious Understanding of Children and Childhood." *JR* 86/4 (October 2006): 549- 579.

Chen, Martha, Joann Vanek, James Heintz. "Informality, Gender and Poverty: A Global Picture." *EPW* (May 27, 2006): 2131- 2139.

Chowdhury, Supriya Roy. "Globalisation and Labour." *EPW* 39/1 (2004): 105-108

Dash, Satya Prakash. "Globalisation and Labour: The Need for Institutional Mechanism." *SA* 58/ 1 (Jan- March, 2008): 59- 72.

Deshpande, Prachi. "Muslims and Dalits as Subalterns". *EPW* 41/34 (2006): 3701-3703

Dietrich, Gabriele. "Why does Post-colonial Feminist Theology Need to Relate to People's Movements." *Asian Journal of Theology* 19/1 (April 2005): 166-187.

Fiensy, David. "Leaders of Mass Movements and the Leader of the Jesus Movement." *JSNT* 74 (1999): 3-27

Louis, Prakash. "Editorial." *SA 54/4* (Oct-Dec): iv- v.

Mehendale, Archana. "Children's Rights: Lessons on Monitoring." *EPW,* 34/ 16 (April 17-23, 2004): 1568-1570

Moltmann, Jurgen. "Child and Childhood as Metaphors of Hope." *ThT* 56 (Jan. 2000).

NCC Review. CXXVI/ 4 (May 2006).

NCC Review. CXXVII/ 7 (Aug. 2007).

Nixon, Rosemary. "Images of the Creator in Gen. 1 and 2." *ThT* XCVII/ 777 (May- June, 1994): 188- 197.

Raja, Maria Arul. "Perspectives of Dalit Hermeneutics." *GJTS* XVI/ 1&2 (Jan. and July, 2005): 23-30.

Ravi, Aparna. "Combating Child Labour with Labels: Case of Rugmark." *EPW* 36/13 (March 31- Arpil 6, 2001): 1141-1147

Sabita Babani, "Child Labour: A Social Problem", *The Economic Times,* (April 10, 1982).

Sakthivel, S and Pinaki Joddar. "Unorganised Sector Workforce in India: Trends Patterns and Social Security Coverage." *EPW* (May 27, 2006): 2107- 2114.

Sarkar, Siddhartha. "Theorizing in Informal Sector: Concept and Context." *SA* 54/4 (Oct-Dec 2004): 359-373

Selvanayagam, Israel "Children Laugh and Cry: Authentic Resources for Christian Theology." AJT 9/2 (1995): 352- 366

Sen, Amartya. "What do we want from a Theory of Justice?" *JP* CIII/ 5 (May 2006): 215-238.

Sen, Ilina. "Adivasis and Tribal Movements: Working Class Perspective in the Informal Sector." *AJTR* XVIII /2 (July-Dec 2005): 66-80.

Shiri, Godwin and Rohan Gideon, "The Plight of Female Child Labourers: A Case Study of Workers in Bangalore." *RS* Vol. 49/50 (Dec 2004-March 2005): 33-71. [co-authorship clarified in *RS* 50/3 (Sep 2005): vi.].

Siddhartha Sarkar, "Theorizing in Informal Sector: Concept and Context." *SA* 54/4 (Oct-Dec 2004): 359-373.

Singh, Avtar. "Child Labour Problems and Prospects: Socio-Legal Measures." *SA* 54/4 (Oct-Dec, 2004): 396-97

Sinha, Shantha. "Child Labour and Education." *Seminar* 474 (Feb. 1999): 14-19.

Swatos, Jr William H and Peter Kivisto. "Max Weber as 'Christian Sociologist'." *JSSR* 30 (1991): 347-362

Tanner, Kathryn. "Theology and Anthropology." *ThT* L/ 4 (Jan. 1994): 567- 579.

Thapar, Romila. "Decolonising the Past: Historical Writing in the Time of Sachin—and Beyond." *EPW* 40/14 (April 2-8, 2005): 1442-1448

Wall, John. "Childhood Studies, Hermeneutics, and Theological Ethics." *JR* 86/ 4 (Oct. 2006): 546.

Weber, Hans-Ruedi. "The Gospel in the Child." *ER* 31/ 3 (1979): 227-233.

DICTIONARIES, ENCYCLOPEDIA AND COMMENTARIES

Clarke, Sathianathan., "Dalit Theology." *Dictionary of Third World Theologies*. Edited by Virginia Fabella and R. S. Sugirtharajah. Maryknoll, New York: Orbis Books, 2000, 64-65.

Devi Laxmi ed., *ECFW* Vol. 4. Lucknow/ New Delhi: Institute for Sustainable Development/ Anmol Publications Pvt. Ltd., 1998, 140-141.

Grassi, Joseph A. "Child, Children." *ABD* Vol 1. Edited by David Noel Freedman. New York: Doubleday, 1992, 904-907.

Hagner, Donald A. "Matthew." *WBC* Vol 33b. Edited by David A. Hubbard and Glenn W. Barker Dallas, Texas: Word Books, Publisher 1998.

Hasel, Gerhard F. "Sabbath." *ABD* Vol. 5. Edited by David Noel Freedman. New York: Doubleday, 1992, 849-856.

Hellwig, Monika K. "Laborem Exercens." *MCE*. Edited by Michael Glazier and Monika K. Hellwig (Bangalore: Claritan Publications, 1992): 489-490.

Martin, Ralph P. "James." *WBC* Vol 48. Edited by David A. Hubbard and Glenn W. Barker. Dallas, Texas: Word Books, Publisher, 1998.

Schippers, R. "Helikia." *NIDNTT* Vol. 1. Edited by Colin Brown. Michigan: Zondervan Publishing House, 1986, 92-93.

Stamps, D. L. "Children in Late Antiquity." *DNTB*. Edited by Craig A. Evans and Stanley E. Porter. Downers Grove, IL: Inter-Varsity Press, 2000.

Thompson, David L. "Yg." *NIDOTTE* Vol 2. Edited by William A. VanGemeren. Grand Rapids, Michigan: Zondervan Publishing House, 1997, 400-02.

Thomson, David " 'ml." *NIDOTTE* Vol. 3. Edited by William A. VanGemeren. Grand Rapids, Michigan: Zondervan Publishing House, 1997, 435- 437.

NEWSPAPERS

The Hindu (Kochi), 20 December 2007.

The Hindu (Kochi), 14 November 2007.

The Hindu (Kochi), 10 August 2007.

UNPUBLISHED MATERIAL

Sathianathan, Clarke, "Dalit Theology: An Introductory and Interpretive Theological Exposition." A paper presented at a symposium entitled *Dalit Theology in the 21st Century: Discordant Voices, Discerning Pathways*, in Kolkata, 13 January 2008.

Shukla, S. P. "Globalisation: Lives and Livelihood." A Lecture delivered at the National Seminar on *Globalization-Life and Livelihood Issues*, held at Kottayam, Kerala, 28 February 2008.

WEBLIOGRAPHY

Azadi India Foundation. *Child Labour in India. http://azadindia.org/ social-issues/child-labour-in-india.html (Children's Day, 2007).*

Bovon, François. "The Child and the Beast: Fighting Violence in Ancient Christianity." *HTR* Vol. 92/ 4. (Oct., 1999): 369- 392. Stable URL: *http://links.jstor.org/sici?sici=00178160per cent28199910per cent2992per cent3A4per cent3C369per cent3ATCATBFper cent3E2.0.COper cent3B2-P (Tue Jan 22 00:31:49 2008).*

Capps, Donald, "Religion and Child Abuse: Perfect Together." *JSSR* 31/1(March 1992): 1-14. *http://links.jstor.org/sici?sici=00218294per cent28199203per cent2931per centper cent3A1per cent3C1per cent3ARACAPTper cent3E2.0.COper cent3B2-P* (22. 1. 2008).

CCCL. A Statement submitted to the National Committee set up by the Prime Minister of India (facilitated by the UNE Division of the Ministry of External Affairs Government of India in preparation for the World Conference against Racism held in Durban, South Africa, in September 2001. *http://www.crin.org/ docs/resources/publications/cccl.pdf.*

Child Labour and Sporting Goods: How Many Children Are Working? *www.globalmarch.org/campaigns/worldcupcampaign/child labour.php.* (15 Sep. 2007).

Edmonds, Eric V. *Child Labour.* http://www.dartmouth.edu/per cent7Eeedmonds/clhbk.pdf (9 Nov. 2007).

Gupta, Himanee. *Reading 'Hinduism' in Moulin Rouge. http:// www.psr.edu/pana.cfm?m=159*

Jamanadas, K. *Caste System contributed to Child Labour in India.*

http://www.ambedkar.org/research/Caste System Contributed To Child Labour In India.htm.

Kaushik Basu, Child Labor: Cause, Consequence and Cure, with Remarks on International Labour Standards.

http://www.essex.ac.uk/armedcon/story id/000413.pdf (9. 11. 2007).

Kee, Howard C. "'Becoming a Child' in the Gospel of Thomas." *JBL* Vol. 82/ 3 (Sep 1963): 307-314. Stable URL: *http://links.jstor.org/ sici?sici=00219231per cent28196309per cent2982per cent3A3per cent3C307per cent3Aper cent22ACITGper cent3E2.0.COper cent3B2-0 (Tue Jan 22 01:00:44 2008).*

Nanjunda D. C. and M. Annapurna, "Small Hands in Silicon City-Bangalore: Some Facts and Experiences at Grass Root Level." *JSS 13/2, 151: http://www.krepublishers.com/02-Journals/JSS/JSS-13-0-000-000-2006-Web/JSS-13-2-000-000-2006-Abst-Text/JSS-13-2-151-156-2006-417-Nanjunda-D-C/JSS-13-2-151-156-2006-417-Nanjunda-D-C-Text.pdf (15 Sep. 2007)*

National Commission for Enterprise in the Unorganised Sector "The Challenge of Employment in India : An Informal Economy Perspective: Vol. 1- Main Report", *http://nceus.gov.in/The Challenge of Employment in India.pdf (May 17, 2010).*

Office of the High Commissioner for Human Rights. *Declaration of the Rights of the Child: Proclaimed by General Assembly Resolution 1386 (XIV) of 20 November 1959.* http://www.unhchr.ch/html/menu3/ b/25.htm (Children's Day, 2007).

Office of the High Commissioner for Human Rights. *Worst Forms of Child Labour Convention, 1999 (No. 182).* http://www.ohchr.org/ english/law/childlabour.htm (Children's Day 2007).

Raman, Vasanthi. *Globalisation and Child Labour. http:// www.revolutionarydemocracy.org/rdv4n1/childlab.htm (Children's Day, 2007).*

UNICEF. *India- Child Labour. http://www.unicef.org/infobycountry/india statistics.html1 (Children's Day 2007).*

Verma, Amit. *Why Child Labour? http://www.indiauncut.com/iublog/ article/why-children-labour/ (15 Sep. 2006).*

Wall, John. "Fatherhood, Childism, and the Creation of Society." (Abstract)*http://muse.jhu.edu/journals/journal of the american academy of religion/toc/aar75.1.html.* (15 Jan. 2008).

Full text in http://crab.rutgers.edu/-johnwall/ (15 Jan. 2008). Originally published in JAAR 75/ 1 (March 2007).

Wall, John. "Human Rights in Light of Children: A Christian Childist Perspective." *JPT* 17/1 (2007): 54- 67. *http://crab.rutgers.edu/- johnwall/ (15 Jan. 2008).*